THE GENESIS OF JOHN

The
Genesis
of
John

A. Q. Morton and J. McLeman

THE SAINT ANDREW PRESS

EDINBURGH

First published in 1980 by
THE SAINT ANDREW PRESS
121 George Street, Edinburgh EH2 4YN

Copyright © A. Q. Morton and J. McLeman, 1980

ISBN 0 7152 0430 0

Printed in Great Britain by
Clark Constable Ltd, Edinburgh

Contents

Preface

This book is an account of a historical investigation of the origins of the *Gospel according to John*. It starts from a recognition of the problems, both internal and in relation to the other three gospels, which this document presents.

To those for whom the Fourth Gospel is a spiritual masterpiece, exposing difficulties and engaging in analysis to solve them will seem to be merely destructive. The authors, however, believe every problem is an opportunity to expand the limits of our understanding and it is in this conviction that the work has been undertaken.

The history of New Testament criticism shows that every advance has come from the deliberate attempt to face and resolve the problems it poses, not from ignoring or minimizing them. Our knowledge about the origin and growth of Christianity would be seriously deficient apart from the critical examination of the differences within and between the four gospels and within the corpus of writings attributed to Paul. It is to those who recognised and investigated such problems, rather than those who accepted these writings uncritically, that all genuine advances have been due; and the process continues.

Since the days of the apostolic fathers when the Fourth Gospel was accepted as worthy to be received and revered by Christians, two assumptions have governed the attitude of scholars to this document. The first is that it is the composition of one man. Even if he drew some of his material from sources which related incidents at which he himself was not present, this material was so informed by his own mind and style that he made it to all intents and purposes his own. In much the same way Shakespeare, for example, absorbed and refashioned after his own image what he drew from Plutarch and Holinshed.

The second assumption is that this book is not primarily an attempt to tell the story of Jesus after the fashion of the Synoptists, but essentially a theological document which expounds by word and deed the meaning of Jesus' life, death and resurrection. The over-riding principle is the significance of Jesus for the world which he became flesh to redeem. The distinctive feature of the book in comparison with the Synoptic Gospels is adjudged to be the deep and mature understanding of the theological implications of his life and teaching for the church and for the world.

These two assumptions underlie the treatment of this gospel from the earliest apprehension that in important respects it was different from the other three. Theophilus of Antioch[1] in the second half of the second century is the first to attribute it to John, 'one of the inspired men'. According to Eusebius,[2] Clement of Alexandria regarded it as 'a spiritual gospel' written by John. Both Theodore of Mopsuestia and Origen, who are representative of the two main patristic traditions of scholarship, the Antiochean and the Alexandrian, agree on its authorship and its theological purpose. Theodore[3] regards it as superior to the Synoptists as history since it comes from a more authoritative source and gives the true chronological course of events. Origen[4] is persuaded that, while it is not in some parts literally true, it sets out more clearly and symbolically than the Synoptic Gospels the supreme theological truth which Jesus came to reveal.

The first assumption has been supported in two ways. First, it has been argued that the style is uniform throughout and it is impossible to distinguish from a literary point of view any difference from beginning to end. The only exceptions admitted are in the Prologue (1:1-18)—a poem on

[1] *Ad Autolycum* 2.22.   [2] *Eccl. Hist.* VI 14.
[3] Theo. 5.14-35; 33, 22-33.   [4] Or. 32.2; 10, 4-6.

the Logos may have been culled from elsewhere (with significant interpolations)—and the last chapter, regarded by many as an addition since an obvious ending occurs at the close of the previous chapter. However, it is argued that here also the style is unchanged and therefore this addition was made by the same author.

Secondly, it is contended that the nature of the material in the Fourth Gospel is such that only someone who was present, or someone dependent on the testimony of one who was present, could have recounted it. Much of this gospel is unknown to the Synoptics and is theologically more profound than they are. It must therefore be traced home to one who had intimate knowledge of Jesus in the days of his flesh and of the ultimate intention of his words and deeds. Since this is what the Fourth Gospel itself claims, there is a *prima facie* case for regarding it as what it professes to be.

Consequently it has seemed impossible for scholars to entertain seriously the notion that this gospel, like the others, is a composite book and that other considerations besides theology have played a part in its construction. It is true that theories have been propounded, as for instance by Delff, Spitta and several others, that perhaps there is a *grundschrift* at the base of the gospel and this has been expanded. Some have thought this *grundschrift* may have been something like *Mark* and this was interpolated by other matter; others have guessed that the base was Johannine and that it was assimilated to the other gospels by material of traditional or Synoptic origin. These speculations, however, have generally been regarded as far-fetched. Those who propounded them have been unable to agree on how the diverse elements should be disentangled. Their theories have depended on their individual subjective judgment.

No satisfactory account of the origin or method of composition of the Fourth Gospel was arrived at. Those who began from the assumption that it is a homogeneous com-

position were forced to conclude that the historical problems
it poses, such as the position of the cleansing of the temple
(2:13-22) and the lack of order in chapters 4 to 6 and 14 to
17, are due to the theological intention of the writer. Those
who began from this theological purpose were *ipso facto* led
to assume that the document is a unity in the sense that it
was conceived and executed by one man.

There is no consensus as to authorship. Some would
maintain that the gospel must owe its origin to the apostle
John. Others cannot accept this conclusion and prefer to
attribute it to a disciple of his, sometimes designated as the
Elder John. It is not ascribed to 'John' till well into the second
century and the first to attribute it to 'John, the disciple of
the Lord', is Ptolemaeus[5], the Valentinian gnostic. But failure to establish authorship has meant that the theological
purpose of the document has received increasing emphasis
with the effect that the tendency has been to explain all problems in terms of theological intention. Thus, for example, the
cleansing of the temple is set early in the book to emphasise
at the outset that Jesus came to institute a new religion
and to annul the old. Discrepancies elsewhere are held to be
insignificant in comparison with the grand design of showing what the incarnation and divinity of Christ mean in the
divine plan of redemption.

The present book begins from the point of view that the
reason why the origin and composition of the Fourth Gospel
have remained an unsolved problem is because these two
assumptions, the unity of the gospel and the commanding
influence of theology in its construction, have not been well
founded. It shows that once these axioms are challenged the
genesis of the book can be understood. It is a compilation of
two distinct sources and a number of its peculiarities are due
not to theological but to editorial considerations.

It is true, of course, that much remains to be said of the

[5] Irenaeus, *Adv. Haer.* 1.8.5.

original intention in publishing the gospel. But this important issue cannot be approached with any hope of solution so long as false assumptions are made about how the book was constructed in the first place. If it turns out that important differences between the Fourth Gospel and the Synoptics are due to the method of compilation, then at these points at least the labours of theologians are as relevant as mediaeval discussions of how many angels can dance on a pin-point. If, on the other hand, we know how a book was made and what were its component parts we have a sound basis for investigating the why and wherefore of its publication.

The problems of the Fourth Gospel are neither trivial nor irrelevant. To solve them one must try to stand beside the person who created the gospel as we have it, a task uniquely suited to a historical investigation.

The reader who is familiar with criticism of the Fourth Gospel will realise the debt which the authors owe to their late teacher, G. H. C. Macgregor. A comparable debt is owed to Professor Sidney Michaelson who created and provided the tools without which this book could not have been written.

J. McL.
A. Q. M.

Part 1

Chapter One

The codex and the New Testament

It is an interesting and important fact that the gospels were coming into circulation when the ancient form of book was about to be superseded by the modern, the roll by the codex. This process took several centuries to complete but the New Testament documents were a formative influence and perhaps they effectively initiated the process.

In the ancient world the chief material for writing was derived from the papyrus plant which grew in the marshes of Lower Egypt and scarcely anywhere else. Strips cut or peeled from its triangular stem were laid vertically, side by side. A second set was placed over the first at right angles and the whole bonded together by blows from a mallet or flat stone to make a sheet which was then dried and polished with pumice. The result was a thin, light, pliable surface which could be written on with a hard reed pen dipped in ink made from carbon black, gum and water.

Papyrus and the manufacture of writing material are described by Pliny the Elder who died in the eruption of Vesuvius in A.D. 79.[1] He tells us that sheets were of standard sizes ranging from thirteen digits to not more than six digits, i.e. from about ten inches to four and a half inches. The largest size, composed of the best material was called *augusta* in honour of the emperor Augustus, and the smallest and coarsest was known as *emporetica* because it was mostly used by merchants for wrapping.

Sheets were pasted together in a row, overlapping each other by one or two centimetres and sold in the form of a roll. As much as was necessary for the purpose in hand (for

[1] Pliny, *N.H.* xlii, 11 ff.

3

instance, a letter, an account, or a receipt) could be cut off.
No doubt single sheets could also be bought in regular sizes
and quantities. For literary purposes the complete roll might
be used up and even extended by pasting on extra sheets. The
result would be more than usually cumbersome. Pliny says a
roll was normally twenty sheets and was never more, but in
this he was mistaken since rolls of over thirty sheets have
been found. Perhaps Pliny is simply stating that the book-
seller sold rolls of that standard size. Nothing prevented a
writer from adding two rolls together if he wished—except
that it would be impractical to handle and consult.

The different sizes of sheets would give room for different
quantities of writing, depending on the width of margins and
the scribe's calligraphy. Exact proportions and consequently
calculations would not be easy. It is reckoned that a roll of
Plato's *Symposium* (*P. Oxy.* 843) may have been about
twenty-two feet long.[2]

The inside (the *recto*) was the normal writing surface.
Here the fibres ran the length of the roll. The outside with
the fibres running vertically (the *verso*) was sometimes used;
generally for different material. Occasionally, writing was
washed or sponged out and the surface re-used.

The writing was in narrow columns running at right
angles to the length of the roll, their length and width and
the size of margins between them varying with the size of
sheet and of the letters. The first sheet, the *protocollon*,
usually ran the opposite way from the rest; that is, its fibres
ran vertically on the inside. It was sometimes left without
writing and as a protective cover for the roll and in some
cases it may have borne the name of the maker or book-
seller.[3]

The change from this form of 'book' to one with pages

[2] L. D. Reynolds and N. G. Wilson, *Scribes and Scholars* (Oxford
1974) p. 3.
[3] E. G. Turner, *Greek Papyri* (Oxford 1968) p. 3.

was of major importance. It probably derived from the convenience of the writing tablet which consisted of a number of wax-coated boards fastened together by a thong or strap and used for short letters, school exercises, notes and memoranda. The Latin term for it was *codex*.[4] The Romans used parchment (animal skin) leaves clasped together as notebooks. They were called *membranae* and were in use at the end of the Republic.[5] Compare *II Timothy* 4:13.

A codex was made by folding sheets to make quires which were then stitched together down the back like a modern book and could be protected by wooden boards on the outside. Perhaps the earliest form was a single quire of, say, five sheets folded to make a book of twenty pages. But beyond a certain number of sheets the single quire book would be very unhandy. The centre pages would bulge out. There is an instance of such a book's pages being trimmed to be even with the edge of the outside pages, with consequent reduction of the writing space on pages towards the centre.

It would soon become plain that quires of a few sheets or of single sheets would bind together more easily, open more readily, and give a uniform size of page throughout the book. The two extremes are seen in *P. Bodmer* XIV-XV (II^{75}), which probably was a single quire codex of thirty-six sheets making one hundred and forty-four pages and is assigned to A.D. 175-255, and the Chester Beatty codex of the Gospels and *Acts* (II^{45}), compiled from single-sheet quires of four pages. There are instances of quires of various sizes from one to eight sheets in one codex. In fact, four sheets making sixteen pages came to be the most common number, just as the most common number of sheets in a roll had come to be twenty. This was called a *quaternio*, whence English 'quire'.

As we have seen, the size of column varied. It depended on the size of page, the width of margins, and the scribes'

---

[4] E. G. Turner, *op. cit.* p. 10.
[5] Reynolds and Wilson, *op. cit.* p. 31.

lettering. In literary texts written by good scribes the length
of line and size of column was generally quite regular. Scribes
were paid by the line and uniformity made for neatness and
easy counting. Some manuscripts show prickings at the side
as a help to accuracy as in an early St. John papyrus codex
(*P. Bodmer* ii[48]). Later, parchment pages were ruled and
some traces of ruling have been found even in papyrus.[6] In
literary texts the line tended to be between fifteen and twenty-
five letters.

Till quite recently it was never doubted that the autographs of the larger New Testament books were written on
rolls. This is not as certain as was thought. The codex form
is now recognised as having been in use earlier than previously imagined. It was taken as axiomatic that the codex
belonged to the fourth century at the earliest, and that
papyrus in codex form dated before then was either misdated
or a surd. This opinion was disputed by F. G. Kenyon,[7] W.
Schubart[8] and Grenfell and Hunt, who all believed that some
papyri in codex form belonged to the second century. More
instances of early date have recently been discovered.

The first mention of literary work in parchment codex
form is in Martial in some poems written in 84-6 and there is
a fragment of a parchment in Latin which is dated A.D.
100.[9] This brings within reach the thought that some of the
New Testament books might have been codices originally.
Reynolds and Wilson express the following opinion, 'The
impulse to change the format of the book must have come
from the early Christians; for while the pagan codex was a
rarity in the second century, the codex form was already
universal for biblical texts.'[10]

[6]   E. G. Turner, *op. cit.* p. 14.
[7]   F. G. Kenyon, *Books and Readers in Ancient Greece and Rome*
(Oxford 1951).
[8]   W. Schubart, *Das Buch bei den Griechen und Romern* (Paris 1934).
[9]   Reynolds and Wilson, *op. cit.* p. 31.
[10] Reynolds and Wilson, *op. cit.* p. 31.

It was C. H. Roberts[11] who provided solid grounds for this kind of conclusion. In 1954 he published an account of the growth of the codex in which he showed that no early text of a Greek New Testament document was written on the *recto* of a roll. All known biblical documents of Christian origin which could be assigned to the second century were codices of papyrus. Since that time, new discoveries have come to light in Egypt which confirm this statement. This means that if the autographs of the New Testament documents were not written on codex (which is not now certain) then they were soon transcribed in this form.

After the invention of the codex form an enormous operation was to take place in which the whole literature of the ancient world was transferred from roll to codex. One consequence was the neglect and ultimate loss of thousands of early manuscripts just as, when printing arrived, whole libraries of codices were superseded. Another consequence was the vast increase of scribal errors both accidental and deliberate which are familiar to the textual critic and to which all copying by hand inevitably gives rise.

[11] C. H. Roberts, *The Codex* (Proc. Brit. Acad. xl, 1954).

Chapter Two

The sizes of the New Testament documents

The advantages of the codex form over the roll form are obvious. The roll was cumbersome to handle; it had to be unrolled and rerolled using both hands. It was liable to accident; many that survive are split down the join or frayed by constant winding and unwinding. It could not hold more than one play or two books of Homer. For purposes of consultation (in the case of religious and legal texts a very important consideration) it had grave disadvantages.

On the other hand, the codex was convenient to handle and could lie open on a desk. It did not require such rough treatment in use as a roll and was easier to consult for quotation or reference. Being written on both sides, the normal codex could hold at least twice as much as the normal roll.

But the codex of a standard size exercised a certain constraint on the writer which is more pronounced than that exercised by the roll. If a written roll were to be divided up into its original sheets, it would be found that many of the edges cut through a column of text. The roll was made by overlapping the earlier sheet on to the later from left to right and the join was smoothed so that the scribe's pen would pass easily from one sheet directly across to the next. In other words, the scribe did not need to consider the join since he could write over it. Consequently, any given sheet in a roll might have one or two complete columns of writing plus any fraction of another column.

The codex, however, contained the same writing area on each page and the scribe had to give attention to this fact.

His space instead of being continuous is now divided into units. But this restriction was also an advantage. The scribe could now calculate beforehand fairly precisely how much space his codex provided for writing. If he was writing a new book and wished to copy some material from another source, as not infrequently happened since there was no such thing as copyright, he could assess exactly how much space such material would occupy. Even if his own book-column were of a different size, it would still be only a matter of simple proportion, such as five columns of the source filling four columns of the book.

Further, if he were writing a one quire book of forty pages, for instance, he could ensure that by the twentieth and twenty-first pages in the centre he had included half the material of the whole book and a similar calculation could be made for a codex of several quires. Naturally the calculation would be easier if the quires were all of the same size. In short, the codex form enabled the writer to keep an easier check on the progress of his book and to plan it in simple quantities, an enormous advantage especially in the case of enlargements and conflations.

As we learn from Pliny, there was a usual length of roll on sale of twenty sheets in perhaps three sizes. It could be underused and the remainder cut off and put to some other use, or it could be extended by additional sheets. The probability is that there were standard sizes of codex. (Some rolls had different sizes of sheets in their form). If so, the whole extent of a codex might not be used but it could not be added to, except possibly by pasting on the outside an extra sheet, a procedure which would normally be avoided since the outside sheet would be prone to accident or loss. This implies some attempt at precision in size on the part of the writer. He is not likely to make or buy a forty page codex for a twenty page book. If this kind of operation is thought unlikely, the answer is that we do this when we decide to send a post-card or letter-card instead of a letter. It is natural that an author should assess whether what he wishes to say can be completed in a further two or ten columns in order to avoid adding on another sheet for the sake of a column of words. The price of papyrus was also a consideration.

Let us now consider the kind of influence that exigencies of space might exert, and whether there are traces of such influence in the New Testament writings. If we find that there are, it will be worth while going on to examine the sizes of these documents.

J. J. Bagley,[1] writing of the daily issue of *The Spectator* which ran from March 1711, to December 1712, says that Addison and Steele and their contributors 'would undertake to write the whole of an issue, much in the manner of those journalists who contract to write a column for a daily paper or weekly journal.' He continues, 'They wrote leisurely and elegantly, almost as if they were writing for the Third Programme, or composing a talk suitable to be broadcast between the two acts of an opera relayed from Covent Garden. But the limitation of their copy was not that it must last fourteen and a half minutes precisely, but that it should fill, but not exceed, four narrow columns on both sides of a sheet of foolscap.'

Limitation of copy or exigencies of space may be enforced for a variety of reasons. A telegram for urgent delivery must convey a message in a fraction of the space the sender might have used in a letter if time were not pressing. The editor of a journal must consider the length of an article in relation to his total space and other articles in the same issue. Predetermined space will affect the material which is to occupy it and the effect will depend on how rigorous the constraint happens to be.

In the case of the roll there was a convenient size, and some have thought that divisions in some parts of the Old

[1] J. J. Bagley, *Historical Investigation*, vol. 2, p. 116 (Pelican).

Testament may be due to this fact. In the judgment of H. J. Cadbury, 'While the length of the scroll and the width of the columns varied, there were conventional or habitual limits.' The constraints of such an indefinite convention, however, would not be very inhibiting and hardly noticeable. If a roll for the book could be anything from twenty-two to thirty-five feet in length, the writer has a large degree of freedom. This was the situation up to the Christian era.

The codex introduced a greater degree of regularity making for more constraint and a more precise concern with space in the book-production business.

If we start from the position of a determinate length of codex, the constraints will vary. The problem will not be so complicated for a writer filling his book with his own composition as for one who is including material from one or more sources at hand. The former has simply to watch the space which is still in reserve; the latter must also decide how much of his source he will use, at which point he should introduce it, and how much space it will occupy in his book in relation to his own material. The former can get into terminal trouble while the latter may encounter internal difficulties as well. These may reveal themselves in forms of dislocation. An epistle like *Galatians* is much easier to fit than, for instance, the *Gospel of Luke* which is planned to include material from other sources.

This does not mean that texts which show no terminal trouble are necessarily in their original state. They may have been copied from roll to codex and at that stage fitted by addition or subtraction to the length. However, if there is terminal trouble, the likelihood is that we are dealing with some miscalculation. Internal trouble is more difficult to detect in some cases and not quite so certainly due to fitting to size but it is still significant.

Terminal trouble will be of two kinds: (a) due to over-running one's space and (b) due to under-using one's space.

The latter will be more likely to occur since a writer is more likely to err on the side of caution. One interesting instance of this is in the third century Chester Beatty papyrus where, as he comes towards the end of his space, the scribe writes in smaller letters to get all his material into the remaining area.[2]

Space left vacant will be liable to be filled by some later hand or by the author at a later time. It is therefore unlikely that a curtailed text will be found in a document which is frequently copied. Thus a few lines or even a column or two at the end which is distinguishable from the main document may be due to using up space left unused in the original. The opposite kind of miscalculation—over-running because of too much text for the space—might show terminal trouble in an abrupt ending.

A number of New Testament books present these features. *Matthew* ends with a few lines summarising the mission of the church and including the trinitarian formula for baptism. Most commentators regard this ending as additional. The Fourth Gospel is thought by many to have finished originally at 20:31[3] (but see below). *Luke* and *Acts* on the other hand are very well fitted in spite of their complicated structure, and the same is probably true of *Revelation*.

In the smaller books, *Romans* has an additional chapter. The doxology in the oldest manuscript and in Origen comes at 16:25-27. In *Codex Alexandrinus* it occurs at 14:23 where it is obviously unsuited, while in the Beatty papyrus it is placed after 15:33. The last position is the most likely, the final chapter being an addition, possibly from another Pauline letter, to complete the codex. *Hebrews* also has a final chapter not by the author of the rest of the text. Some commentators believe it was added to give epistolary status to the original discourse.[4]

---

[2] *P. Bodmer*, xiv-xv.
[3] See, for example, C. K. Barratt's commentary, p. 18 f. (1st ed. S.P.C.K.).
[4] See, for example, A. C. Purdy in *I.B.*, vol. 11, p. 592.

Of the opposite kind of feature, over-running space, *Mark* provides an obvious instance, cut off at 16:8. Someone added 16:9-20 in the conviction that 16:8 was not the original ending. Ten or twenty lines may have been attached to complete the book which became detached and lost. This kind of miscalculation is less likely to occur and therefore this instance is all the more significant.

Turning now to internal trouble due to splicing or interposing material and resulting in dislocations and displacements, these also may be affected by the need to fit text to space. They are most likely to occur in composite works as a result of difficult decisions about how much of a particular source to use and where it should be introduced.

If we accept the Proto-Luke hypothesis, we have a classic example of the kind of problem the author faced and its successful solution. He extended his primary source by adding a new beginning and selections from a Markan source and brought the total out to the required length. To do this he had to make a neat adjustment in the third quarter of the book. He realised he would be a number of columns short and made this good in parables in chapters 15 and 16.[5] (These are included by Streeter in Proto-Luke. It is a strong argument against his position that without them Proto-Luke is the same size as *Mark*).

There are signs of internal adjustment in *Acts* also. Stephen's speech in chapter 7 contains an extremely long discourse which can be lifted out without harm to the narrative. Furthermore, Paul's conversion is related three times without much variation or additional detail. Perhaps the author did not want his book to end except where it did.

The epistles also show adjustment to length. *II Corinthians* is composite and it is not clear whether it contains part of two or four original letters. *Ephesians* has the appearance of

[5] MacGregor and Morton, *The Structure of Luke-Acts*, chap. 3 (Hodder and Stoughton).

an extended version of *Colossians*, while *II Peter* gives
another version of material in *Jude*. In shorter documents it
is all the more likely that size was prominent in the mind of
the writer. *I Peter* is in two halves, editorially joined and
coming out at the same size as *James*.

It is doubtful if any hypothesis can explain these anomalies which does not include the constraints imposed by a
predetermined amount of space. We therefore go on to ask
whether there is any kind of relation between the sizes of
New Testament documents which might confirm this hypothesis and for the purpose we use Souter's *Novum Testa-
mentum Graece*.

It might not be thought surprising that *Luke* and *Acts* are
about the same size since they are compiled by the same
author and are sometimes referred to as volumes one and
two of the same work. But it is remarkable that two hand-
written documents of over 16,000 words should be within
200 words of each other if not by design; and that a third,
Matthew, should run to very near the same length. Kenyon[6]
gives the figures in pages of the Chester Beatty Codex as
Matthew $49\frac{1}{3}$, Luke 50, Acts $50\frac{1}{3}$. In the *Codex Sinaiticus*
these three books total 271,232 letters. The average is
90,414. Three quarters of this is 67,813 and the Fourth
Gospel adds roughly to 70,000 while *Revelation* is about
45,000, half the big three. Thus there is a possible 4-3-2
series. *Mark* appears to have been written on a different size
of page, but Proto-Luke would run to the same size as we
have observed.

When we turn to the epistles, *Romans* runs to 677 lines of
Souter, *I Corinthians* to 647 and *II Corinthians* plus
Galatians to 666, a considerable regularity in hand-written
text and a convenient tripartite division of the genuine letters
of Paul. *Philemon* and *Colossians* are 160 and 159 lines
respectively and *James* and *I Peter* are 178 and 177. The two

[6] G. F. Kenyon, *op. cit.* p. 51 f.

small Johannine epistles are twenty-four lines each while *Jude* is just over double at fifty-one. The largest books (*Matthew*, *Luke* and *Acts*) are eighty times the size of the smallest or a possible fourscore pages of the same size.

It is very difficult to regard all these coincidences as chance-generated. What they have in common argues a relationship in the sizes and quantities of the material on which they were written and this in turn means that the documents as we now have them have been copied on the codex form of manuscript.

There is a second stage in the formation of the New Testament canon which is equally notable from the point of view of size. The four Gospels, *Acts* and *Revelation*, *I Corinthians* and *Romans* appear to have been large enough to maintain a separate existence. The next step is the gathering of smaller documents into convenient book form. We have seen that the four Pauline epistles are capable of being contained in three manuscripts of equal size—*Romans*, *I Corinthians*, *II Corinthians* with *Galatians*. The remaining New Testament books can be gathered into three books of conventional size with the exception of *Hebrews* and *II Peter*.

Ephesians, *Philippians* and *Colossians* add to 552 lines in Souter which is within three lines of half of *Mark*. The Valentinians appear to have used the first four Pauline epistles and *Ephesians*, *Philippians* and *Colossians* according to Souter.[7] *I* and *II Thessalonians*, *I* and *II Timothy*, *Titus* and *Philemon* add to 637 lines, *James*, *I Peter*, *I*, *II* and *III John* and *Jude* add to 645 lines. This means that these five gatherings of documents, namely, (1) *Romans* (2) *I Corinthians* (3) *II Corinthians* and *Galatians* (4) *I* and *II Thessalonians*, *I* and *II Timothy*, *Titus* and *Philemon* (5) *James*, *I Peter*, *I*, *II* and *III John* and *Jude*, do not vary by more than thirty-three words in 100 lines from a mean of 654 lines of Souter.

[7] A. Souter, *The Text and Canon of the New Testament*, p. 167 (Duckworth).

As regards *Hebrews* and *II Peter*, it is easy to understand why these were not bound up with others at the same time. The history of the canon shows that *Hebrews* long remained a matter of dispute as to authorship. Indeed, in the western churches doubts appeared from time to time, even if its quality was regarded as apostolic. Hilary of Rome and Pelagius both wrote commentaries on thirteen epistles of Paul, omitting *Hebrews*. Souter[8] tells us that in *Codex Claromontanus*, *Hebrews* is obviously a later addition. This explains why it appears at the end of the Pauline corpus, the rest having been gathered into five books before it was finally agreed that *Hebrews* should be included in the canon.

There is no trace of *II Peter* before A.D. 170 and it also was excluded from the canon till Eusebius' time. The Catholic epistles were presumably collected into one at a later time than the collection of Pauline letters and *II Peter* was added to the former as *Hebrews* to the latter. Last of all came the other book on which opinions remained divided for a longer time than for the bulk of the New Testament writings, namely *Revelation*, which was able to stand on its own.

[8]   A. Souter, *The Text and Canon of the New Testament*, p. 28.

Chapter Three

The search for objective criteria

The study of the four gospels has generally been carried on in two separate compartments—the examination of the first three, *Matthew*, *Mark* and *Luke* conjointly and then the examination of the Fourth Gospel separately. There is a good reason for this. The first three are aptly called synoptic because they share a similar viewpoint and deal with the same theme in the same way. In all three Jesus speaks in a simple and distinctive manner; in all three his character develops with his experience, and in all three there is a common pattern of a Galilean ministry followed by a climactic last week in Jerusalem.

There are, of course, discrepancies and divergencies. The relation between the Synoptics is much subtler and more complex than it was assumed to be when the explanation of their origin was that both Matthew and Luke had a copy of the canonical form of *Mark* before them as they wrote. But the differences can be seen as the consequence of having independent accounts of the same sequence of events. Many of the differences are due not so much to any variation in the actions or words of Jesus but to the effect of his words and deeds on friends and enemies.

Over against the Synoptics stands the enigmatic Fourth Gospel, a presentation of Jesus' life and words which is not amenable to the same synoptic pattern, either with regard to the person of the principal character or to the sequence of events in which he was involved. Here Jesus delivers long speeches in a style which has been characterised as grandiosely monotonous. Here the cleansing of the temple which the Synoptics set in the last week of Jesus' life is found near

17

the beginning of his ministry, and the Fourth Gospel recounts not one but four visits to Jerusalem. The Synoptics
follow the last meal (a Passover meal to them, but the Fourth
Gospel places it on Passover eve) with the institution of a
permanent celebration. The Fourth Gospel omits this but
precedes the meal with the ceremony of washing the disciples'
feet.

The Fourth Gospel therefore raises acute historical questions. If the book is correct in its account of the incidents of
the last night of Jesus' life, the Synoptics have omitted an
important incident; if they are correct then the Fourth
Gospel has failed to record an event of primary significance.
Such discrepancies mean that if history is being written by
one it is being rewritten by the other.

The Fourth Gospel is also distinct in that it presents internal problems which have led to the suspicion that it may not
be in its original order. Since the days of Tatian, around
A.D. 170, it has been noticed that some rearrangements of
the text make it easier to read. The oldest and simplest
change is to read the gospel in the order that interchanges
chapters 5 and 6. In chapter 4 Jesus is on one side of the sea
of Galilee, in chapter 5 he is on the other side, and in chapter
6 he makes the crossing which connects the incidents. Similarly it gives better continuity if 6:14-24 follows chapter 5
and 7:25 follows 7:13. A number of such transpositions are
generally accepted. Some of them involve lengths of text
which are multiples of a unit variously thought to have been
a column or a page and many theories have tried to explain
the 'disorder' of the gospel as the consequence of an accident
to the original manuscript.

In addition, the Fourth Gospel has its quota of textual
difficulties. It begins with a prologue which is generally
thought to have been incorporated from another source. It
has the detached paragraph, 7:53-8:11, of the woman taken
in adultery, which occurs in some good manuscripts but not

in others. The last chapter is thought by many to be a later addition. In the *Codex Sinaiticus* the text originally stopped at 21:23 but the scribe erased his colophon, copied 21:24,25 and then repeated his colophon. This erasure is the only textual evidence for any alteration in the gospel. The complete absence of any history of change is a formidable objection to many theories which subject the text to a series of transformations.

If there is any one problem which might be the key to all the others it is that of the unity of the gospel. On this there are three main attitudes. The first is that the gospel is a unity and the problem exists only in the minds of the gospel's detractors. The second is that the manuscript has suffered textual dislocation for one reason or another. The third is that the gospel is not a homogeneous composition but the result of conflation.

Many critics believe that the author left his book in the condition in which it now exists or that he or some other at a later period added the prologue and the last chapter to what is essentially a document produced by one mind. Dodd regarded the anomalies as simply the 'phenomena of composition'. W. F. Howard believed that for some reason the writer was unable to revise his book and it is an unfinished production. Barrett sees no need for explanation. There are certain 'roughnesses' but the style, vocabulary and theological outlook show it to be the work of a single author except for the prologue and epilogue.[1]

Theories that the present form of the text is the result of an accident-prone history are based on the notion that the original fell into disorder or suffered damage, and an editor, not the author, made what he could of the chaos by placing the parts in what he conceived to be their original order. The ingenuity of these theories is the best argument against them. If the history of the gospel has been as fortuitous as they

[1] *Commentary*, p. 20.

suppose, rational criticism is hardly possible. The critic hopes to discover order and purpose but here is a tale of disorder, transposition and the wayward impulse of an editor who at one moment compels admiration for spiritual insight and at the next is rolling dice. Derangement theories do acknowledge one truth, namely, that there are irregularities in the structure of the gospel which it is the business of the expositor of the gospel to explain.

The late Professor G. H. C. Macgregor was a leading exponent of the view that the present gospel is the result of enlargement.[2] The weakness of his case was that he had to unravel a mechanical problem with theological tools. In his collaboration with Morton,[3] thirty years after his original commentary, the textual consequences of the constraints of production were considered. This was a step forward. Where it fell short was in the failure to produce sufficient evidence of diverse elements in the conflation and to explain some of the features which resulted from it.

Most of the attempts to discover sources in the Fourth Gospel have proceeded on one or other of two assumptions. The one is that the basis of the gospel is a primary document akin to the Synoptics, and that this has been enlarged by the interpolation of material special to the Fourth Gospel. The other is that the original was distinctively 'Johannine' and that it was worked over by someone who wished to bring it into line with the synoptic tradition. From Delff to Garvie these two lines of investigation were pursued, with various modifications, depending on the scholar's notion of the date, provenance and intention of the document.

To some extent, Bultmann departed from this pattern when he delineated three primary sources: a 'book of signs', mostly miracles; a series of 'revelation discourses' consisting largely of speeches by Jesus which were gnostic in tendency,

---

[2] *The Gospel According to St. John*, London, 1931.
[3] *The Structure of the Fourth Gospel*, Edinburgh, 1961.

and a 'passion narrative' which might or might not be akin to the first source. Bultmann shared with others the conviction that the editor's intention was to bring the work into alignment with the life and teaching of the church and with the received gospels.

What can be said of these attempts to delineate sources is first of all that their persistence shows that scholars cannot be satisfied that the solution to the gospel's structural constitution has been found, and that their diversity emphasises the fact that the criteria used in attempts at a solution have not been adequate. Because of the lack of agreement in attempts to delineate sources it has been easier to conclude that the premiss is fallacious and the work must therefore be homogeneous. Consequently, many recent commentators have given scant attention to authorship except in relation to the question of the gospel's authority in theological terms.

R. H. Fuller has pin-pointed the reason for this lack of agreement in theories of derangement and composite authorship and the consequent lack of interest in the possibility of tracing sources. 'The trouble is that there has never been any precise agreement on re-arrangement. F. R. Hoare[4] attempted to furnish such an objective criterion by a calculation of the exact numbers of letters per page to the original autograph. Unfortunately, however, he had to assume part of what he set out to prove.'[5]

This perceptive comment is worthy of consideration. Käsemann criticised Bultmann's division into sources as too dependent on his notions of what the evangelist ought to have said. His solution was devised in accordance with his subjective ideas of what might have happened in the process of composition from a theological point of view. This criticism is relevant to all attempts hitherto to distinguish sources, with the two exceptions of Hoare and Morton, and

[4] *The Original Order and Chapters of St. John's Gospel*, Burns Oates, 1944.
[5] *The New Testament in Current Study*, S.C.M., 1963.

their work is the origin of the attempt to find non-subjective criteria for the solution of the problem of authorship in the Fourth Gospel.

These two attempts were quite independent. Morton had no knowledge of Hoare's work when he collaborated with Macgregor. Both worked with the same notion of column or page size but Hoare's work postulated breaks in the text (open spaces) which vitiated his experiment, while Morton, in addition to using column size, was the first to apply modern techniques of stylometry on the problem as a primary criterion. The present book uses both these objective criteria with the benefit of all the developments and research which have taken place in the last fifteen years. It will therefore be appropriate to say something of the nature of these criteria by way of introduction to their use in this book.

Stylometry has shown immense development in recent years but, unfortunately, most New Testament scholars remain either ignorant of it or sceptical of its application to New Testament problems of authorship. They are content to rely on literary and theological expertise in dealing with such questions and are largely unaware that statisticians, literary students and classical scholars are already familiar with the help it can offer on such questions. There is an unwillingness to admit that questions of authorship in the New Testament are not theological and a distrust of statistics and the usefulness of the computer as a labour-saving device of incredible speed and accuracy.

To the literary critic, style is a concept which depends on the distinctive manner in which a particular writer expresses his thoughts and which is apprehended rather than comprehended by the literary critic in such a way that he can make a judgment of quality, based on general considerations about mannerisms, constructions and vocabulary which he has trained himself to detect. He may also use his subjective judgment on the subject matter of the text before him to help him form a conclusion as to authorship. The theologian proceeds on the same principles using his knowledge of the development of theological ideas to help him to discriminate between one document and another or between different parts of the same document.

It does not need to be stressed that both operations depend to a large extent on the subjective estimates of an individual mind, that different authorities may come to diverse opinions and that the conclusions of both literary and theological criticism may be challenged and usually are. Hence the success of many a literary hoax and the fact that theologians frequently have to revise their notions about the date and extension of theological concepts (witness the impact of the Dead Sea Scrolls).

What is necessary is the discovery of some criterion which reduces the dependence at the outset on individual subjective judgment and does not depend on arbitrary factors which catch the eye simply because that is the kind of thing the critic has been taught to look for. Such features form a very small percentage of the text, they can easily be imitated and they can certainly mislead. Stylometry approaches these questions by analysis of the complete text and draws its conclusions from those structures which no one would think of imitating and which are independent of subject matter but which truly indicate the habitual moulds which a writer uses when he puts his thoughts into words.

The indicators of style in this sense which enable one writer to be distinguished from another are not those which attract the interest of the literary connoisseur or the accomplished theologian but those which reveal the patterns in which he orders his thoughts, irrespective of subject. Fortunately, these are the frequent words that for other purposes are regarded as insignificant and yet make up the bulk of a composition. 'What', asks one theologian incredulously, 'can one learn from a word like "and"?' The answer is, 'A great deal if there are sufficient of them.' Of course, it is not simply a matter of counting. Stylometry has been developed to a highly skilled science. But the point being made here is that it begins from objective facts which none can dispute, and not from subjective surmises.

As regards the column structure of a document, this also is an objective statistical fact. If columns have an equal size, they have an average number of letters which admits of little variance. It is true that manuscripts and column sizes are not uniform and those used by the writer of the archetype of the gospel are not known. For instance, of three manuscript pages recently examined one has an average of twenty-five letters per line and twelve lines per column, a second eighteen letters by twenty-two lines and a third fourteen letters by twenty-two lines. Columns of the large *Codex Sinaiticus* hold an average of six hundred and seventy letters, much the same as *Codex Vaticanus*. These, of course, are comparatively late for our purpose, but the number of letters per line averages fifteen. *Codex W* of the Freer Gospels has a column per page running to eight hundred and fifty letters while a codex of the Paul Epp. (*Papyrus 46*) from the third century, also one column per page, runs to about seven hundred and fifty. Originally columns were narrow, running from ten to twenty letters and probably two columns to a page. This may be about the measure of the archetype of the Fourth Gospel but it is not possible to be sure on such a point.

It may well seem that little use can be made of our knowledge that manuscripts were written in columns since such uncertainty remains about size and number, but one or two considerations will show that this is not so. We have already seen that there is a remarkable precision in the sizes of New Testament documents. The scribe is a craftsman. He has worked out for his own convenience the best way to design and execute his manuscript. He knows what a codex of a particular size will hold. In copying verse scribes sometimes made a mark, usually a letter, at the end of each one hundred lines and a total at the end. This would be the basis of calculation of the fee due to him and no doubt similar rules of thumb were used in copying prose. The column is the natural and most convenient unit for the scribe's purposes.

Consider also the fact that although in writing the scribe did not divide his material up into chapters, paragraphs and sentences, as the modern habit is, nevertheless he thought in these terms as we do, and the convenience of ending a section at the end of a column and beginning a new section at the opening of a new column would not have escaped him. Particularly if he is using different sources from which to copy, the column is the obvious unit of measure and he is likely to have designed the shape of his book in advance in terms of columns. It is true that, supposing two documents were being used in a conflation, they might be of columns of different sizes from that of the new book. This however would only be a matter of simple proportion, as that four columns from source A will fill three columns of the book.

Now these facts are important for the reason that they are objective and that, although there are no markings in the text to indicate the size of column directly, it is possible for us to detect where a logical section ends and another begins and therefore to experiment with possible sizes of column since we can assume that some columns will end at such points. For this purpose we can use a modern edition of the text with some assurance. A comparison of the Greek texts of the Fourth Gospel produced by, for instance, the British and Foreign Bible Society (1904), A. Souter (1910) and Aland, Black, Metzger and Wikgren (1966) will show that there is remarkable unanimity among them about the places at which a change of subject or topic should be indicated, either by a new paragraph or (in BFBS) by a space between sentences.

One further fact may also by of use. The *Apocalypse* is half the size of *Luke* and *Acts* while the Fourth Gospel is midway between these two sizes. This gives a progression of 2:3:4. If *Luke* was planned in quarters, the likelihood is that the Fourth Gospel was planned in thirds or sixths. What can be done, therefore, is to prepare a letter count of the gospel by computer. It amounts to 71,335 letters including the *Pericope Adulterae* which usually appears as 7:53-8.11 and amounts to eight hundred and twenty-two letters. Most commentators are agreed that this pericope does not belong to the original, so the gospel runs to 70,513 letters. Using a modern paragraphed text we can experiment with a view to using the regularity of the column structure as an aid to discovering the structure of the gospel. This, however, must go hand in hand with stylometric considerations.

Chapter Four

The constraints of codex and compilation

All over the British Isles there are to be found numbers of megalithic monuments. To describe these is impossible; they contain anything from a single stone to several hundred stones. The stones are of different sizes, shapes and kinds; the patterns in which they are arranged vary from a single marker in an isolated position to complex lines and curves spread over large sites. Anyone bold enough to suggest that underneath this variety lay some regularity was, until recently, laughed to scorn. What regularities can possibly arise from a group of objects which differ in every element by which they can be described? Any claim that regularities existed was patently absurd. So it was widely believed, until Professor J. A. Thom presented a paper to the Royal Statistical Society and followed it with two books.[1]

What Thom had done was to make an accurate physical survey of a number of monuments (previous surveys had left much to be desired), and to apply to the results some mathematical principles. What emerged was something not apparent to the naked eye, or to common sense; it was that these monuments had been built, using a common unit of length, to act as different kinds of calendars. The type of calendar determined the nature of the monument. There are still some uncertainties about these monuments, but scholarship has gone on to new ground and the introduction of scientific techniques has transformed yet another discipline.

[1] The larger units of length of megalithic man. *Journal of the Royal Statistical Society* A 127, 527, 1964.

Thom's case has many parallels. When C. B. Williams submitted a paper to the *Journal of the Royal Entomological Society*, the president, a fellow of the Royal Society, returned it with the comment that they could not allow logarithms to appear in their journal. Williams lived not only to become president of the Society and a fellow of the Royal Society, but to see the whole subject changed from simple description to statistical analysis.

The same pattern is always repeated. A subject is practised unscientifically, even when it is said to be a descriptive science in its own right. The scholars established in the field are intelligent and articulate; from a long experience they have endorsed conclusions which arise from their critical position. Along comes a stranger whose qualifications are suspect. (Thom was a retired professor of engineering and no archaeologist; Williams was a young man with limited experience). Strange principles are applied that lead to radically different conclusions. The established scholar can accept the conclusions no more than he can accept the man who puts them forward. The scholar is confronted by new evidence which he quite literally, cannot see. When he catches a glimpse of what kind of evidence it is he will tend to misunderstand it and so misrepresent it.

Sometimes the misunderstanding is due to the unfamiliar nature of the evidence, more often it is the result of the common psychological reaction to information which undermines one's position. Out of sheer exasperation it is deliberately misunderstood and misrepresented. An example of this is a paper on the authorship of some New Testament epistles submitted to the *Journal of Biblical Literature*. It was rejected on the grounds that it was full of computer jargon and therefore much more suited to a computer journal. In fact the word 'computer' was not used in the paper. Not one term used in computing occurred in the paper and the statistics employed are those expected of sixteen-year-olds in British schools. A critic has no defence against a new technique of which he has no experience and in which he has no standing. Like the savage confronted by the aircraft, he can only rattle his weapons and shout at the sky. It would be ingenuous to expect him to welcome the change.

The study of the New Testament manuscripts is still in the pre-scientific phase. That is not to say that some scholars have not used scientific techniques in particular problems; it is to say that no theory has been propounded which embraces all the books of the New Testament. To show how far this is true one need only argue that some physical factors have influenced the formation of the Gospels and Epistles. Any such suggestion meets with an immediate rejoinder in one or other, or in both, of two forms.

The first is the assertion that while theological, literary and cultural influences have repeatedly been shown at work in the creation of the New Testament texts, no one has yet shown that any physical constraint has operated in a comparable manner. This objection conveniently overlooks the difficulty of getting an argument about physical factors published. A study of *II Corinthians*, a letter constructed under severe physical restraints, was sent by the late G. H. C. Macgregor and one of the authors to the *Journal of Theological Studies* many years ago. It was rejected as having no theological content, hardly surprising in a paper written to show that the key factor in the construction of the Epistle had not been theology but necessity.

A reader employed by the Clarendon Press commented on the same argument as 'papyrus sheet mania'. This remark raises the second objection. It is suggested that if any standard textbook of papyrology is consulted (a convenient pair are those of E. G. Turner: *Greek Manuscripts of the Ancient World*, Oxford, 1971; and *Greek Papyri*, Oxford, 1968), it is clear that manuscripts came in all sizes and shapes, in all kinds and conditions, in all formats. They varied in every descriptive detail and so any suggestion that they exhibit regularities is patently absurd.

This is exactly the situation which faced Thom at the start of his work on the megalithic monuments. No theory can be published while it is held to be, *prima facie*, absurd and the evidence of the absurdity is the solid-seeming evidence of common sense and the eye of any reader. But Thom was producing evidence of a new kind and evidence made manifest only by powers of mind. The question which Thom raised for these monuments is the same one as is being raised here for the New Testament manuscripts. If there is complete freedom in the choice of material and design for these books and letters, how is it that there are regularities in their sizes? To some extent scholars have already faced this question. No one would be surprised that the *Gospel of Luke* and the *Book of Acts* are almost identical in length. They have been regarded as two parts of the same work executed by a single author in the same period. But what of the *Gospel of John*? Written in another place at a different period and probably by another method, it turns out to be three-quarters of the length of *Luke* and *Acts*.

Thom explained the regularities of monuments by two principles. First, was a resolve to build a calendar of one kind or another; second, came the principles for constructing such things. The explanation offered here for the regularities in the books and epistles of the New Testament is precisely parallel. Someone wanted to write a book. Having taken the decision, he then used the rules which enabled him to construct the book he wanted to write.

The starting point is to recognise that there are two limits to the size of manuscripts. At the lower end of the scale there is an ultimate constraint; if a manuscript is no more than a scrap of paper with a few words on it, it will be found inconvenient to keep and use and the scrap will be combined with other notes into something more easy to handle and consult.

This commonplace principle can be illustrated from the gospels where short parables are gathered together and various collections of one kind and another show up clearly. At the other end of the scale there is the other ultimate constraint: the manuscript becomes too large, or too expensive, to be practical. This limit may well vary from time to time and place to place and be different for the collector of artistic productions and the purchaser of a student's text, but it is not at all surprising to discover that the three largest books of the New Testament contain about 90,000 letters, i.e., about 20,000 words.

The texts of the New Testament also show that the smallest manuscript which could lead an independent existence would seem to have just over eleven hundred letters in it. There are two epistles of this length and a number of the larger paragraphs in the gospels, notably the longer parables, are also about this size. But between these limits, if the evidence of common sense is to be accepted, there is no reason to suppose that any number of the texts should show any relationship in their size.

This means that the first step to be taken is that taken by Thom, to show that there is some regularity for which an explanation is required. The two situations, of the megalithic monuments and the New Testament manuscripts, are not just similar on the surface. Thom had sets of measurements so alike that identical design was the only explanation, exactly as in *Luke-Acts*; he had others, as we have *Matthew*, rather removed from these measurements and so questionably connected with them. Not surprisingly, the piece of mathematics used by Thom applies here. Table 4.1 shows the number of letters in the New Testament books in the Greek text of Aland, Black, Metzger and Wikgren (London, 1966) and the result of applying to the Gospels, *Acts* and *Revelation*, the analysis adapted by Thom. The conclusion is that if these are taken to be a set of manuscripts whose length

TABLE 4.1

The lengths of the New Testament texts

Book	Number of letters in book	Notes
A. *The major books*		
Matthew	89,940	
Mark	55,332	To 16:8
Luke	95,804	
Acts	95,696	
John	71,335	Including 7:53-8:11
Revelation	45,961	
B. *The Epistles*		
Romans	34,936	To end of 15. 32,235
I Corinthians	32,754	
II Corinthians	22,263	
Galatians	11,080	
Ephesians	11,999	
Philippians	7,994	
Colossians	7,882	
I Thessalonians	7,402	
II Thessalonians	4,037	
I Timothy	8,856	
II Timothy	6,525	
Titus	3,724	
Philemon	1,563	
Hebrews	26,368	To end of 12. 24,384
James	8,814	
I Peter	9,049	
II Peter	6,066	
I John	9,508	
II John	1,132	
III John	1,118	
Jude	2,576	

The Greek text is *The Greek New Testament*, edited Aland, Black, Metzger and Wikgren (London and New York, 1966).

TABLE 4.1 (*continued*)

Book	Number of letters in text	
	Observed	Calculated from series*
C. *The major works of the New Testament* *as components of a series*		
Luke	95,804	95,300
Acts	95,696	95,300
Matthew	89,940	95,300
John	71,335	72,400
Mark	55,332	55,300
Revelation	45,961	47,600

* The calculation follows Thom 1967, C. is 1.40.

increases in simple proportion, the differences between the observed letter-counts and the values predicted can be accepted as chance variations. This is not proof that such a series exists, only that there is no objection to starting with this working hypothesis.

In tables 4.1 and 4.2 are set out the numbers of letters in all twenty-seven books of the New Testament and in the twenty-one orations and nine epistles of Isocrates. Table 4.1, which covers the New Testament, is divided at 40,000 letters. The division corresponds to the two different kinds of book which the New Testament contains. The larger books are compilations, the smaller books are compositions. The epistle is a homogeneous literary form; all parts of the text are consistent with each other and with the whole since the single root of the epistle is the mind of its author. Even if the writer of an epistle has some notes prepared or a quotation or two written out, making up and setting down the text are parts of a single operation, even when the writing down is delegated to a scribe. But the redactor of a gospel is not composing a text; he is assembling material from many minds and making a sequential narrative from them. He is

TABLE 4.2

The Orations and Letters of Isocrates arranged in order of size

Orations	Number of letters in Oration	Epistles	Number of letters in Epistle
15	97,395	2	6,939
12	86,967	9	6,206
4	59,130	6	4,653
5	46,974	4	4,378
8	43,718	7	4,240
6	33,876	8	3,599
7	25,070	1	3,023
9	24,891	3	2,194
18	20,196	5	1,572
10	20,139		
3	20,053	T.	36,556
17	18,156		
14	17,923		
2	16,126		
16	15,557		
1	15,523		
19	15,482		
11	14,856		
13	7,241		
20	5,994		
21	5,632		
T.	610,079		

The text is that of Mathieu and Bremond (Bude, Paris, 1962).

acting as the modern editor does and when he composes a linking passage or rewrites a group of short passages into a larger unit, his role is secondary and the text still bears signs of its diverse origins.

Because there are two different kinds of books there are two different critical problems. Of an epistle one asks, 'Who wrote it, in what circumstances was it written and with what intention?' Of the composite book one asks, 'Who assembled this book, from where did he get the component sources, and what purpose did his work achieve?'

Another reason for making a division within the New Testament is that there is evidence that some epistles have been grouped together for publication and if this is indeed the case then the figures in table 4.1 would not be relevant to a simple test of seriation such as that used on the major books.

Table 4.2 records the letter counts for all the orations and the epistles of the famous orator Isocrates. Oration One is not his, though it may be a compilation with which he had some connection. Isocrates was the model speech-writer. A joke was made about Plato that he first followed Socrates and then followed Isocrates. But because he was a model for style and pattern of argument, Isocrates' works were carefully preserved, not subject to the revision so often required to adapt the sentiments of a master to the changed situation of later generations. Isocrates is singularly free from what A. D. Winspear has called 'the loving distortions of discipleship'. He wrote for the unparalleled period of sixty-five years and so has been made the subject of a study of the effects of time on individual style.[2]

There is no possible doubt that Isocrates wrote on papyrus rolls. The title of each oration and the *prooimion* indicate that the text was written on the roll form of book.

Tables 4.1 and 4.2 show a simple common feature. The range of size is much the same in both. The New Testament runs from 1118 letters to 95,804. Isocrates runs from 1572 to 97,395. This does suggest that the largest convenient size of book was just under 100,000 letters. At the lower end of the scale the agreement is quite good, bearing in mind that

[2] Things Ain't What They Used To Be, Michaelson, S. and Morton, A. Q. in *The Computer in Literary Studies* (University Press, Cardiff 1976).

II and *III John* may not ever have led a separate existence and the shortest book to lead such a life might well have been *Philemon* with 1563 letters in its text as against the 1572 of Isocrates' *Fifth Epistle*.

The second feature of the two tables is the different grouping of the texts. Sizes can increase in two ways, by simple increments or by proportional increments. The difference between the two graduations is easy to illustrate. Suppose a text had ten pages; one page can be added to make the total eleven, another can be added to make it twelve and so on. In each case the actual increment is the same but it becomes a smaller and smaller proportion of the whole with each successive extension of the text. This is simple increase. Now suppose that the text of ten pages is extended by ten pages, this doubles the size to twenty pages. The next extension in this series would be to double it again from twenty to forty pages. This is proportional increase, each step is an increase of one hundred per cent.

In practice, proportional increases are much smaller than one hundred per cent and are achieved by a combination of larger pages as well as more pages. There is reason to expect that texts, books and paper sizes should be proportionate, as for most of history they have been so. Since the introduction of printing this has certainly been so. When books were written and reproduced by hand there was more choice. The actual choice open to the writer depended on the form of book. Papyrus rolls were sold ready for use. If the size was convenient for the author, all he had to do was adopt a format and write his text in it. If, however, he found the roll a constriction, all he had to do was either to take his scissors and snip off any section unused or to take his paste and add a section to his roll. In other words, one would expect to find in a corpus written on rolls some reflection of the common sizes of rolls but wide variations around these common and convenient lengths. It would be unlikely that very large or very small texts would show any regularities for these would be the result either of constructing a roll to suit some particular situation or of using some of the off-cuts generated by the natural variation in writing rolls.

A text written on a codex is not so easily adapted. This text is written on quires of folded sheets stitched together. If you cut off the last pages you will endanger earlier sheets by exposing an edge or by unbalancing the forces on the binding. To add anything less than a quire is also to disturb the binding. The codex is a form which can be readily enlarged in steps measured in quires. The weak spot in the codex is its spine with its bindings and to offset this the size of page would be increased when the number of quires reached a practical limit.

To sum up, we can expect to see little or no difference in short texts written on rolls or in codices. Whether or not a short epistle is classed as roll or codex may mean nothing more than whether it was rolled or folded when it had been written. But in the large and medium sizes of text we would expect differences between the forms to appear. Written in codices, texts will have regularities in the larger books; the larger the texts the clearer they will be. Written on rolls, texts will show no regularities in larger sizes but cluster around the common sizes of roll.

This is exactly what we do find in tables 4.1 and 4.2. In Table 4.1 we have a major series with 47,600 letters, 55,300 letters, 72,400 letters and 95,300 letters. The permissible variations are wide but that reflects the fact that the minimum number of points needed to define a straight line is three, straight lines can always be drawn through any two points, and there are only four sizes represented. However, chance is a reasonable explanation for the variations that do appear.

There are other regularities in the sizes of the shorter texts, some of them striking, but, as was said earlier, these are not of the same kind; they are the result of gathering more than one text into a larger unit.

In Isocrates the situation is quite different. His two longest texts have 97,395 and 86,967 letters. If these two are the first elements in a series, this would continue at 77,656 letters, 69,341 and 61,916 letters. In fact, the next text has 59,130.

A noticeable feature is that there are two groups of texts around 15,000 and 20,000 letters. In the first group are *Oration 11* with 14,856, *Oration 19* with 15,482, the spurious *Oration 1* with 15,523, *Oration 16* with 15,557 and *Oration 2* with 16,126 letters. This group averages 15,509 letters and the variation is 653 letters, 4.21%, above the average and 617 letters, 3.98% below the average.

Three orations are near to 20,000 letters, *Oration 3* at 20,053, *Oration 10* at 20,139 and *Oration 18* at 20,196 letters. The three average 20,129 letters and the variation is 67 letters above the average and 76 below, a range of 0.33%. If these two groups were part of a series the next members of the series would be 33,907 and 44,007 letters.

It is clear from the comparison of the two tables that the ordering of the texts is quite different. In Isocrates the larger texts are isolated while the medium lengths are in two separate groups. This structure corresponds to the physical constraints imposed by the nature of the papyrus roll. The major books of the New Testament on the other hand form a series and illustrate what is convenient for the user of a papyrus codex.

The final point to note in table 4.2 is that it is the spurious *Oration 1* which lies nearest of all to a predicted length; it has 15,523 letters compared with a group average of 15,509, a difference of only 14 letters in 15,509, 0.09%. It is not without significance that this work is composite. When a writer selects a roll or codex on which to write his text he no doubt chooses a size which accords with his purpose and which allows him to cover his subject in the detail which he wishes to include. He will therefore measure the progress of his text by counting pages or columns but only to make sure that all is going well. At the mid point of his text he should be about half way through his composition. As he nears the end he will adjust his text to ensure a fitting and tidy conclusion. It would be reasonable to expect that there is a general relation between the progress of his composition and the progress of his text, but like the motorist who has an adequate supply of fuel, he pays attention only to preserve his peace of mind.

The writer whose task is the compilation of a text from various sources is in a very different position. His sources will be in differing formats and he must measure the relationships between the component parts and the whole book with some precision. If he has the freedom conferred by using a roll he can readily adjust the roll to suit the text but if he is compiling a codex he must adjust his text to the codex. He must measure much more carefully than the writer who is either writing a free composition or making a compilation on a roll. The corpus of Isocrates shows that compositions can vary as much as four per cent above and below an average length but the one compilation in the corpus stays within 0.09% of the average size.

The major books of the New Testament can be expected to show the full effects of planning. They are compilations and they are written for the unforgiving codex form. All this has emerged from a simple general physical examination of the two sets of texts, the New Testament and the Orations of Isocrates.

Part 2

Chapter Five

The structure of the Fourth Gospel

The starting point of what it would be convenient to call the Macgregor–Morton theory of the gospel was a simple comparison of the Greek text of all four gospels. The comparison is repeated in more modern form and on a newer text in Table 5.1. Of the four, the *Gospel of John* has the shortest words and sentences but these are made into the longest paragraphs. The brevity of the words and sentences in *John* can be readily explained. It contains a large number of particles, connectives and enclitics which, together with a preference for the simplicities of speech, produce the results shown in the table. But it remains the striking feature of the Fourth Gospel that its materials should aggregate into larger blocks than that of the other gospels.

The next step in the Macgregor–Morton theory was to look at the length of the paragraphs in the four gospels and

TABLE 5.1

A comparison of the four gospels

Gospel	No. of letters in average word	No. of words in average sentence	No. of words in average paragraph
Matthew	4.94	14.11	122.2
Mark	4.93	13.85	123.3
Luke	4.98	14.94	132.7
John	4.56	13.36	190.7

In this table the paragraphs are taken to be marked off by the English titles of Aland, Black, Metzger and Wikgren.

this showed that the feature which made the Fourth Gospel such a striking exception was that it contained a larger proportion of long paragraphs, then defined as more than thirty lines of Souter's text, and that a comparison with the other gospels showed there was an increase in the proportion of such paragraphs when *Mark* was used by *Luke* and *Matthew*. Some of the higher proportion in *Matthew* and *Luke* when compared to *Mark* might be due to the larger scale of these gospels but this would not explain why *John* had more such paragraphs than either since it is a shorter text. In the first three gospels the proportion of long paragraphs was some indication of the structure of the book; the enlargement from *Mark* to *Matthew* and *Luke* had created more such paragraphs. If this was true then the Fourth Gospel could be a compilation rather than a composition. This was Morton's first contribution to the initial hypothesis.

The pattern of paragraph lengths was also used to eliminate a traditional red herring, the theories of textual dislocation. The removal of a page or sheet from a text will necessarily break two paragraphs into four and even if some of the junctions in the new position were happy enough to enable the two fragments at each junction to become a new paragraph, this would not often be the case. If the text had suffered anything like the number of dislocations required to make such theories possible, then there would be in *John* a plethora of short paragraphs created by the transpositions. Not only are such short paragraphs absent; there is in the text this high proportion of long paragraphs which makes transpositional theories even less credible.

Macgregor started from this point. He took the long paragraphs and attached to them such others as were, in his opinion, part of the same source. When he had done this he found he had six panels which showed remarkable regularities in size and spacing. Morton then argued that it was the insertion of these panels into a continuous text which had created the canonical form of the Gospel and so given rise to many of the problems presented by it.

At that time the argument was developed under some restrictions since removed. A model was used to illustrate the construction of the gospel. The model was based upon Souter's Oxford text of the New Testament and the unit was one line of the printed text. The advent of the computer has made possible much more accurate and flexible models in which the unit is the number of letters in the text, the unit in which it was written. The second restriction under which the work was done was that no techniques then existed by which the authorship of a piece of Greek text the length of any of the panels could be determined in comparison with another piece of about the same length. Since then, stylometry has advanced far enough to make a useful contribution in such situations.

Lacking these aids Macgregor faced two insoluble problems. He could distinguish short redactional passages which he believed had been inserted by the editor responsible for the present form of the text, but he was not always able to decide if these should be included in his calculations or left out. The accuracy of the model was not sufficient to enable this dilemma to be resolved. His other problem was that, lacking the means by which the authorship of short sections of Greek text can be determined, he did not feel able to do anything but accept the contents of the panels as having come from a single source. By itself this would have been no crippling handicap but it meant that he could not decide if any material congruent with the panels existed outside them or whether any material had been interchanged between the panels and the remainder of the gospel. The model suggested a simple structural theory and any attempt to modify this would have led critics to reject the model and with it the foundation of the new theory. So the theory was propounded and published. In the years that remained to him Macgregor published no further views on the Fourth Gospel. Morton always argued that the Macgregor–Morton theory was about 90 per cent right and that a few adjustments to it would make it as good a theory of the origin of the gospel as we are likely to have.

The genesis of what can be called the McLeman–Morton theory was McLeman's dissatisfaction with some aspects of the earlier hypothesis. It seemed to be right in many particulars but the discrepancies were irksome. So ten years after the first examination a second was begun. Available to the authors were better tools and better techniques. The Greek text was in a computer and better models based on the counting of the letters in the Greek text could be made and also be easily adjusted. Also to hand were techniques which could resolve some of the problems of the authorship and origin of the components of the gospel. Between them these aids would do much to resolve the dilemmas which Macgregor had found impossible to handle.

A model of the text is a simple aid to visualising the situation which confronted the writer of the gospel. Whatever form of book was used, a roll or, more likely, a codex, the text would have been laid out in columns. To understand the problems which arose as the text was being written it helps if we take a number of columns, a number consonant with the surviving manuscripts from the same era, and divide the text into units of columns. The score was widely employed as a unit of counting and measure so a model of the gospel will be one with a few score columns of text; in this instance 180 columns. These columns may be too large or too small to be an accurate reproduction of the original but for comparisons within the text all that is required is accuracy of proportion. This is not affected by the size of columns used in the model. It will matter no more than measuring a building in yards or metres; as long as one system is consistently applied no harm will come.

The text of the Fourth Gospel laid out in 180 equal columns would have 391.74 letters per column. No column can have this number and most columns will have different numbers of letters in them. It is not very difficult to estimate by how much any sequence of columns will vary in content. All that we need to know is the number of columns in the sequence and the difference between the largest and the smallest columns in the sequence. Neither of these pieces of information can be derived from the original, but one, the number of columns in the sequence, can be taken from the model and, in making comparisons within the gospel, this will not mislead. An assumption has to be made about the second figure but it can be checked against the few contemporary manuscripts which do exist.

At the end of the 1st century A.D. a column of just under 400 letters could have been written in a variety of shapes. If it was a narrow column it might have had forty lines of ten letters. If it was a broad column it would have been around twenty lines of twenty letters. A writer, especially if writing into a codex, is not likely to leave out of a column the equivalent of a whole line of lettering. An omission on this scale would be striking. So we can take as a guide the rule that the most compactly filled column and the most loosely filled one would be unlikely to differ by more than two whole lines of text, in this case about forty letters. In comparing a number of columns in sequence the range of variation will then be plus and minus twice the difference between largest and smallest, forty letters, divided by the square root of the number of columns in the sequence. Nineteen times out of twenty the chance variation in a sequence of twenty columns will not exceed $(2 \times 40) \div \sqrt{20}$ letters per column, so in the whole sequence about twenty times as much, i.e. 180 letters out of a total of 8,000. This is a reasonably liberal allowance and most sequences of twenty columns will differ by less than this number of letters. But the calculation does suggest two things, namely, that when differences larger than those predicted do appear some cause other than chance variation is required to account for them, and, similarly, if differences much less than this, say less than one quarter of the number, appear, it suggests that the normal operations of chance have been suspended. If sequencès of twenty columns differ by fewer than about forty letters, it must be concluded that the regularity is unnatural.

It has been suggested earlier that a writer putting a text into a codex will tend to make the major sense divisions of the text and of the manuscript agree. At the mid point of his story he will be about half-way through his writing. This suggests that a useful exercise is to size off the gospel into any sections that it might appear to possess. The principle of division is very simple. The text is divided regularly; if it is halved then each half will have in it 35,257 letters. The text is examined to see if a paragraph ends near to that point. Such an ending will be accepted as a division of the text only if it lies within the predicted limits of chance variation from the spot and if the adjacent paragraphs lie outside these limits. When this is done in the Fourth Gospel the book falls into six sections as shown in table 5.2.

Just as the traveller setting out for Oxford from Edinburgh first looks at the small scale map which show the relation of the two cities and the run of the roads and motorways, then takes up the detailed map which shows him how to clear the suburbs of the city and emerge on the main roads south and west, so it is useful in studying the structure of the gospel to begin with a small scale general diagram which shows only the large features of the conflation which created it. Later this will help with the fine details as they come under scrutiny.

One of the complications of Johannine studies has been the nomenclature used by its critics. Sections are attributed to the evangelist, the disciple, the elder, the witness and so on. Each of these has its origin in some view of a source but

TABLE 5.2

The main divisions of the text of the Gospel of John

Section	Text of section	Number of letters in section	Number of letters in average column in section
1	1.1-4.38	11,693	389.8
2	4.39-7.15	11,743	391.4
3	7.16-10.18	11,646	388.2
4	10.19-13.20	11,748	391.6
5	13.21-18.14	11,915	397.2
6	18.15-21.25	11,768	392.3

The highest average is for section 5, 397.2 letters, the lowest for section 3, 388.2 letters, a difference of plus and minus 4.5 letters, 1.1%, of the average for the two sections taken together. Section 5 is anomalous as shown in figure 5.1 which shows the order statistics for the six sections. Only the average of section 5 does not lie on or near the line which passes through the grand average for all six sections. Further evidence of the existence of the anomaly is found when the sections are taken in pairs and sets.

can be quite misleading in other contexts. It is better to adopt a completely neutral system and to number the components in order of size and so separate the structure of the book from hypotheses of the origin of the components. The largest source is called J1, the next smaller J2. No meaning other than an ordering in size should be read into, or out of, this nomenclature. Redactional material is labelled R and sub-divided as R1 and R2. In this case R1 denotes a redaction within a source and R2 a redaction which united sources. Again the description is purely structural.

The gospel in the model used fills 180 columns. Exactly half come from J1 which totals 90 columns. J2 runs to 78 columns and there are 12 of redactional material. In this count the text of 2.12-25 is put as J1 since only its present position is redactional; it has been shifted from its natural position in the passion narrative.

Each third of the gospel has in it 30 columns of J1. The simple relation of the six sections can be seen by running through them from the last to the first. Sections 5 and 6 are mirror images of each other. Sections 4 and 3 are also mirror images while the only difference between sections 1 and 2 is that the same amount of J2 text is inserted into both but in a single sequence in section 1 and in two sequences in section 2. The structure shown in outline in figure 5.2 could hardly be simpler.

Just as it helps to have a simple small-scale diagram to enable the broad structure of the gospel to be seen before the details are examined, it may be useful to have a summary of the theory as it affects all six sections before going into the details of any of them.

Table 5.2 contains a number of striking features. First to be noted is that the first half of the gospel, from 1.1 to 10.18, contains 35,082 letters. The second half has 35,431 letters in it. The difference is 349 letters, a variation of plus and minus 175 letters and the calculated chance variation for 90 columns is plus or minus 372 letters. So it would appear that the mid point of the gospel occurs at a sense division of the text. Further division reveals that the gospel is in six parts as set out in table 5.2 and these exhibit some fascinating regularities. Sections 1, 3 and 5 add to 35,254 letters, sections 2, 4 and 6 add to 35,259 letters, a variation of plus or minus 5 letters, 0.007%. To attribute this precision to chance would be absurd; it would be difficult to match the two halves of a book with such precision using all the helps which are available to contemporary craftsmen.

The regularity in sections 2, 4 and 6 is particularly striking; 11,743 letters, 11,748 letters and 11,768 letters. The average is 11,753 and the variation of plus 15 and minus 10 letters are proportions of plus 0.13% and 0.09%.

FIGURE 5.2

The structure of the Gospel of John *in broad outline*

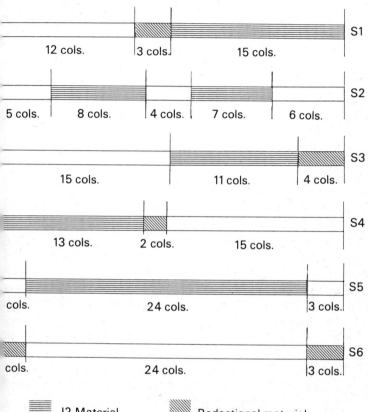

| J2 Material | | Redactional material |

Sections 1, 3 and 5 add to almost the same total as the contents of sections 2, 4 and 6 but there is more variation between them. It could therefore be argued that it is the variation which is natural and its absence from sections 2, 4 and 6 which requires explanation or that a precise design has

FIGURE 5.1

The order statistics of the average number of letters per column in the six sections of the Gospel of John.

$\bar{x}$ denotes the average for the whole Gospel.

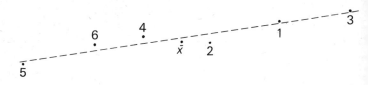

been blurred by some factor operating in sections 1, 3 and 5, particularly in section 5. This dilemma can be resolved by resorting to order statistics. The average number of letters per column for all six sections and for the whole gospel are calculated and arranged in sequence from the highest to the lowest or the other way round; it matters not at all which order is used. Reference is made to a set of statistical tables in which the intervals of order statistics are given[1] and a graph is drawn as in figure 5.1. If the figures are of the same kind, the points will lie close to and be separated by the line drawn through the grand average for all the sections. If they are not of the same kind or if there is an outlier among them, this will appear from the graph. Figure 5.1 shows that five of the six sections are regular and section five is an outlier. This technique merely draws attention to the anomaly; it has nothing to say about the cause of the anomaly.

The conclusions to be drawn from table 5.2 are that the *Gospel of John* has been designed in six sections, each on average of 11,752 letters; that three sections, 2, 4 and 6 have preserved this precision of measurement, averaging 11,753 letters and varying from it by only 10 and 15 letters in over

[1] The Statistical Analysis of Experimental Data, J. Mandel (New York 1964).

11,000 but sections 1, 3 and 5, while averaging 11,751 letters, show a larger variation. It is also to be concluded that the variation in sections 1, 3 and 5 concerns section 5 which has 164 letters more than the average. The reason for this may be the necessity to balance sections 1 and 3 against section 5 as 1 and 3 have 58 and 105 letters less than the average.

The Fourth Gospel is therefore a book which is written with a totally unnatural degree of precision in the planning of its sections. There is one major anomaly in section five but even this is much less than the natural variation in writing a text of this length. The anomaly is large only in contrast with the precision of its companions. This structure should not be understood as being a book with one anomaly pushed into it with the resulting deformation of two earlier sections. What the structure does show is that the Fourth Gospel is a conflation of what can be described as an unparalleled precision and that within it one major anomaly has at once emphasised the remarkable precision of the sub-divisons of the text and also demonstrated that an anomaly of only 174 letters has repercussions throughout the text.

It might seem natural at this point to return to the Macgregor–Morton theory to show that the panels as delimited by rounding out the long paragraphs explain the present form of the gospel as due to a conflation of sources. But the differences between that theory and the revision in the McLeman–Morton theory make this undesirable. The first difference has just been demonstrated, namely, the clear division of the gospel into six parts. The second has been mentioned earlier. It is that the sources of the gospel may themselves be composite and so it is not likely that any simple comparison of one part of the text against another will yield useful results at this stage.

The procedure adopted by the authors is to start with a hypothesis of what the sources of the gospel were and how they were conflated, then to explain the complications of order and structure as the consequences of applying general principles to the particular situation of the Fourth Gospel. Only when this has been done is there a simple and consistent theory to be propounded. This theory can then be validated by a number of statistical tests which show that the component sources cannot be accepted as the work of a single writer. This sequence of exposition and of testing is most easily followed after an examination of the six sections of the gospel.

Chapter Six

The conflation of the Gospel

To any observer trained in a physical science the most striking feature of the gospel is that it has six paired sections. Sections 1 and 2; 3 and 4; 5 and 6, are, with slight modifications, mirror images of each other. This suggests, and examination of the evidence supports the suggestion, that the sections were planned and written in pairs. This in turn means that the compilation of one section is affected by what has been written in the previous section or what it is planned to write in the following section. The description of the conflation will have to take account of this pairing.

A second feature of the sections of the gospel is that they show clear signs of two units of measurement, one appropriate to the J1 material and the other appropriate to the J2 material. In the first survey of the gospel the authors used a model which had thirty columns per section. In this model the J2 material showed clear regularities. At the end of the examination the authors decided that this model was difficult to reconcile with the fact that the most likely format for the gospel was one in which sheets had been folded to make four pages and so the number of columns per section should be divisible by four. They therefore changed to a model of twenty columns per section. In this model some features of the J1 material were more apparent than they had been in the thirty column model. But much of the regularity of the J2 material was hidden. They then decided that the exposition of the conflation should be based upon a model of thirty columns per section and the question of the possible format of the original copy of the gospel should be looked at separately.

At this point only one conclusion is drawn which is that, whatever the format of J1 and J2, they were very nearly in the ratio of 2:3, two columns of J1 are about as much as three columns of J2. This ratio is reflected in a number of places through the conflation.

Sections one and two

Section one: 1.1-4.38 (Illustrated in figures 6.1 and 6.2)

The agreement of the written text and the mathematical model is so close that it cannot be explained by chance. The largest discrepancy between the text and the model is a deficiency of thirteen letters in a sequence of 2,326, 0.56%, between 1.31 and 2.11. If the sequence is taken as starting at 1.1, then the difference is of seven letters in 4,670, 0.15%.

Within this first section of the gospel there are three major problems. The first concerns the prologue to the gospel and the prose comments which have been inserted into it, (1.1-18). The second arises from the present position of the cleansing of the temple (2.12-25) and the third is the introduction of the J2 material starting at 2.26.

For the configuration of the prologue and the prose comments there are three possible explanations. Both could be original and belong to an early stage in the creation of the gospel and so have arrived at the redactor in their present form. Neither could be original and both have been added by the redactor who compiled the gospel and so added them at a late stage of the conflation. One or other could be original and the other added to it to accomodate the pair to the present form of the gospel. There is evidence both positive and negative which bears upon these questions though much of the evidence is not to be seen if attention is confined to

FIGURE 6.1

The conflation of the gospel illustrated by a model

SECTION ONE

TEXT

1.1	1.30		2.11	2.25		4.3		4.38

	2,344		4,670	5,842		8,963		11,693

LETTER COUNTS

Number of letters in section 11,693.
Average column 389.8 letters.

TEXT	OLC	EC	ELC	D1	COLC	CELC	D2
1.1-30	2,344	6	2,339	+5	2,344	2,339	+5
1.31-2.11	2,326	6	2,339	−13	4,670	4,677	−7
2.12-25	1,172	3	1,169	+3	5,842	5,847	−5
2.26-4.3	3,121	8	3,118	+3	8,963	8,965	−2
4.4-38	2,730	7	2,730	0	11,693		

OLC number of letters in text. ELC calculated number of letters in text. D1 difference between OLC and ELC.
COLC cumulative total of letters in text, CELC cumulative total of calculated numbers of letters in text. D2 difference between COLC and CELC.

this part of the first section of the gospel. The relation of the prologue and the prose comments is shown in figure 6.1a. There are two patterns to be noted. The first is that the prologue and the prose comments run to 1,117 letters and the prose comments are near to one quarter of this; they are in all 273 letters and one quarter would be 279. So the prose comments have extended the prologue by about one third.

The second regularity is that the first of the comments has 168 letters, the second has 105. Both are simple multiples of 21 letters, 8 and 5.

Neither the end of the prologue at 1,117 letters, nor of the prologue without the prose comments, 844 letters, is a significant fraction of the gospel as it now stands nor of the J1 source as it has survived in the gospel. The prologue and prose comments were combined but not to provide a front porch for the gospel if that porch ends at 1.18. The relationship of the two requires an explanation which goes beyond this section.

FIGURE 6.1.a

The structure of the prologue of the gospel
(The diagram is illustrative and not to scale.)

VERSES IN TEXT

LETTERS IN TEXT SEQUENCE

The two prose comments are of 168 and 105 letters. These add to 273 letters, one quarter of the whole would be 279 letters.

Of the second problem within the first section, the presence of the cleansing of the temple thus early in the gospel, only two things need be said at this point. The first is that the account of the cleansing fills exactly three columns in the model, one tenth of the section. The difference between the model and text is three letters in 1,169. This must argue that the passage has been carefully fitted into position at this point. The second thing to note is that the narrative would fit naturally into position in the passion sequence of the gospel, as will be seen in a later section, and so can have been readily transferred from there to its present position.

This raises the question as to why it should be so transferred. The following text begins the J2 material and the major story is about a Samaritan woman. It is not easy to see how such a story would fit into sequence with Jesus in Galilee. But if he is brought up to Jerusalem, then he could interview Nicodemus and return to Galilee through Samaria. It may be objected that to do this is to do violence to the geographical and chronological sequence of the gospel. It would indeed do so if the gospel were designed above all to have and to show such sequences. But a compiler who has been as free with the story of the last night of Jesus' life can hardly be thought to be a slave of historical sequence.

It would appear that all three major problems of the first section of the gospel have a common origin. All flow from the decision to start J2 material at the mid point of the section and to prepare for it. The first section of the gospel shows all the signs of a well-planned and carefully executed conflation. The two sources alternate in a simple sequence. The section contains 11,693 letters, just sixty letters fewer than the grand average for all six sections. It could be argued that this suggested a designed length for the section of 11,753 letters but somehow or other sixty letters got left out. Or it could be argued that this section was designed to hold 11,693 letters. This is an example of the kind of dilemma which in Macgregor's day could not be resolved. He could mark off a number of passages within the major sources but was never able to decide if these anomalous passages had been in the sources or were introduced by the redactor to make the sources a proper fit to the new gospel which he was compiling. A redactor can add, or omit, a few lines at any time and in any position simply by leaving out, or putting in, text of exactly the same amount. If he is copying a narrative and finds that a reference in it to some event which now precedes it would enhance his story, he can add a few details simply by omitting others. An example of this kind of adjust-

ment is seen in verses 39-42 of chapter 4 where a short
passage, described by Macgregor as lacking historical foundation, has been rewritten in the light of what now precedes
it in chapter 4. Another example of a slightly different kind
is in verses 1 and 2 of chapter 4. These are a conglomeration
which makes little sense. From the model it can be seen that
these verses come at a major junction within the J2 source.
It is the need to end this block and prepare for the next
which has produced this compound conflation and union of
sources.

In other instances, 13.36-38 for example, Macgregor was
in no doubt. He was sure that this passage had been added
in the final redaction for it illustrates one of the primary
interests of the redactor, the desire to reduce Peter's standing
and importance. But generally Macgregor had no method
which would separate passages which had played a part in
the creation of one of the sources of the gospel from a
passage which had played a comparable role in the redaction
which created the present form of the gospel.

TABLE 6.2

*Two alternative hypotheses compared in the first
section of the* Gospel of John

Position within section, at end of column	Observed number of letters	Two alternatives and the differences between the alternatives and the observed progress			
		E. 11,693	Diff.	E. 11,753	Diff.
6	2,344	2,339	−5	2,351	+7
12	4,670	4,678	+8	4,701	+31
15	5,842	5,847	+5	5,876	+34
23	8,963	8,965	+2	9,011	+48
30	11,693	11,693	—	11,753	+60

One simple way to determine the role of any passage is to look at it in an error diagram. An error diagram is a continuous record of the progress of the written text against some theory of its compilation. For example, we want to look at two alternatives, that the first section of the gospel was designed to contain either 11,693 letters or 11,753 letters. Within the section the sources change at the end of columns 6, 12 and 15. For a section designed to have 11,693 letters, the predictions and the observations agree closely. At the end of column 6, five letters have been written more than the expected number. By the end of column 12 there are eight letters more in the prediction than the performance and at the end of column 15 this has shrunk to a difference of five letters in 5,847. Closer agreement is hardly to be expected.

When the comparison is repeated with expectations calculated from a section of 11,753 letters, each junction lags behind the expectation and the lag steadily increases until it reaches sixty letters at the end of the section. It is quite possible that sixty letters can be omitted from a text; they can even be left off right at the end; but the effect of such omissions is not at all what we see here. Examples of these patterns of omission will be seen later in the gospel but the conclusion is that the first section was designed to have 11,693 letters and was executed to do so with remarkable precision.

Section two: 4.39-7.15.

Careful fitting of the first section is essential to the progress of the conflation. If the relationship of the component sources is accurately established, the design will be simplified. If the first section were to be irregular, or the sizes uncertain, difficulties could well arise in later sections. From this point of view the design of the first section can be regarded as eminently successful. An immediate consequence of the success of section one appears in section two. This second section runs from 4.39-7.15 and has in it 11,743 letters. In the first section J2 material filled half the section, 15 columns in the model, 5,851 letters. The other fifteen columns of the first section held 5,842 letters. The second section has two sequences of J2 material, 5.9(b)-5.47. 3,063 letters and 6.22-54, 2,774 letters making a total of 5,837 letters in both J2. It would appear that the amount of J2 in both the first and second sections is the same but it is in a single sequence in section one and divided into two in section two. The division will present no problem for no matter where it is made, the two sequences together will fill fifteen columns.

The section starts with J1 material which runs for 1,943

FIGURE 6.2

The conflation of the gospel illustrated by a model

SECTION TWO

TEXT

4.39

| 5.9a | 5.47 | 6.21 | 6.54 | 7.15 |

| 1,943 | 5,006 | 6,646 | 9,420 | 11,743 |

Number of letters in section   11,743
Average column   391.4 letters

TEXT	OLC	EC	ELC	D1	COLC	CELC	D2
4.39-5.9a	1,943	5	1,957	−14	1,943	1,957	−14
5.9b-47	3,063	8	3,131	−68	5,006	5,089	−83
6.1-21	1,640	4	1,566	+74	6,646	6,654	−8
6.22-54	2,774	7	2,740	−34	9,420	9,394	+26
6.55-7.15	2,323	6	2,349	−26	11,743		

Note 5.9b-47 plus 6.22-54 is 5,837 letters, 15 columns contain 5,871; 6.1-21 plus 6.55-7.15 is 3,963 letters, 10 columns contain 3,914 letters.

letters; five columns of the model would hold 1,957 letters. Then comes the first J2 passage which ends at a point no less than sixty-eight letters from the end of a column. The succeeding J1 passage runs for 1,640 letters and ends, with the precision we have come to expect of the conflator, with column 17. The difference between observed and expected totals is eight letters in 6,646. This reflects the fact which was earlier noted, that as the two J2 sections add to the contents fifteen columns, he can divide them up with complete freedom; at the end the total will be right.

When he has reached the end of section two the conflator has grounds for satisfaction. He has completed one third of the book, sixty columns. He has filled exactly half of these from J2. Having established the relationship of the sources in the first section, he puts the same amount of J2 in both sections but uses his freedom to separate the two passages within the second section of the book.

From the first two sections of the conflation some deductions can be made. The J2 material is in six parts and contains in all 30,360 letters. Table 6.1 shows how these parts are placed throughout the gospel and how all but the second and third parts are exact multiples of the J2 column size and if the second and third are taken together they become such a multiple. This suggests that the J2 material has been placed in suitable positions and any adjustments needed have been made in the J1 source. That this is the case can be seen from a number of features of the text. One is the regularity of the J2 material in sections one and two; it is 11,688 letters in two parts of 5,851 and 5,837 letters, a variation of only seven letters; while the other material in the same two sections is 11,748 letters in the two sections of 5,842 and 5,906 letters, a variation of thirty-two letters.

It will not have escaped the watchful reader that the contents of section one at 11,693 letters is very near to the amount of J2 at 11,688 letters, while the contents of section

TABLE 6.1

The J2 sequences in the gospel

Site and text of sequence	Observed number of letters in sequence	No. of columns	Expected no. of letters in sequence
S1 2.26-4.38	5,858	15.0	5,840
S2 5.9b-47 6.22-54	3,063 ⎱ 5,837 2,774 ⎰	7.9 ⎱ 15.0 7.1 ⎰	5,840
S3 8.48-9.41	4,277	11.0	4,283
S4 10.19-11.46	5,040	13.0	5,061
S5 14.1-17.26	9,355	24.0	9,344
Totals	30,367	78.0	30,368

two at 11,743 letters is close to the total from the other sources of 11,748. This difference between the length of the sections reflects a difference between the sources which has been preserved in the compilation. It means that the contents of any section could be predicted as:

$$\frac{N1 \times 11,748}{30} + \frac{N2 \times 11,688}{30}$$

where N1 and N2 are the number of columns filled by copying from J1 and J2. To make a prediction about the first two sections using the information based on the actual count of these sections would add nothing to our knowledge of these sections, but predictions made for later sections will have some value.

At the end of section two, one third of the book is complete and equal parts of it have come from the two major sources. Redaction has taken two forms, 273 letters have been written as prose comments into the prologue and one section of J1, 1,172 letters, has been moved forward to its present position at 2.12-25. Of the seventy-eight columns of J2 material thirty have been placed in position. This is about the rate required to put it all in place before the redactor comes to the final sequence of the gospel in which insertions are likely to become more difficult to make by reason of the close texture of the narrative. If he decides to put all of J2 in before the final section of the six, he will have to put a little more in sections three to five than he has been doing, but only enough to raise the average from fifteen columns with J2 in each section at the end of section two, to make the average for section three, four and five, sixteen columns per section.

THE SECOND PAIR OF SECTIONS
Section three and four

Section three: 7.16-10.18, 11.646 letters.

In the first part of section three the redactor arrives at an important decision. The decision may well have been made earlier but only at this point does it become visible. When he reaches the end of chapter 7 he omits 7.53-8.11, the story of the woman taken in adultery. The omission offers the only logically consistent explanation of the manuscript evidence. From the earliest copies of the text the paragraph is missing but in later ones it has been restored. This is explicable only if it was known that the story once had a place in the text and had been left out. The memory was that it had come at the end of chapter 7 but the slight uncertainty about its precise place has already been referred to.

FIGURE 6.3

The conflation of the gospel illustrated by a model

SECTION THREE

TEXT

7.16 7.44		8.47		9.41	10.18
2,348		5,878		10,155	11,646

LETTER COUNTS

Number of letters in section   11,646.
Average column   388.2 letters.

TEXT	OLC	EC	ELC	D1	COLC	CELC	D2
7.16-44	2,348	6	2,329	+19	2,348	2,329	+19
7.45-8.47	3,530	9	3,494	+36	5,878	5,823	+55
8.48-9.41	4,277	11	4,270	+7	10,155	10,093	+62
10.1-18	1,491	4	1,553	−62	11,646		

For the conflation the omission poses no problem. It only requires a decision about whether or not it should be replaced by an equivalent amount of other text. The alternative which was chosen by the redactor will soon become clear, but it should be noted that he has added 273 letters to the prologue, almost precisely one third of the 822 letters in the omission. He has 549 letters in hand.

The structure of section three could not be much simpler. The first half, fifteen columns, are filled from J1 and contain 5,878 letters. Then follow just over eleven columns filled from J2, 4,277 letters, and finally just under four columns of redaction, 10.1-18. The whole section has in it 11,646 letters. By the rule used for predictions it should have: $\frac{15}{30} \times 11,748$ letters plus $\frac{11}{30} \times 11,688$ letters plus 4 columns at an unknown rate. The first two components in the calculation seem in order. J1 would have 5,874 letters by prediction and has

5,878 by actual count; J2 would have 4,286 letters by prediction and has 4,277 by actual count. Only the 1,491 letters
in the final columns is out of line with the precision which
has so far been such a feature of the conflation. It is however
entirely compatible with the view that the redactor preserved
the structure of the components in the new book. J1 and J2
are not identical and so 15 columns in the book filled from
J1 contain 5,874 letters while the same 15 columns filled
from J2 would have 5,844 letters. Columns filled from a
redactional source would be expected to preserve some trace
of their origin. In this case the columns contain 1,491 letters.
Filled from J1 they would have 1,566 and filled from J2
1,558 letters. This may seem a large discrepancy but it is
so only in contrast with the remarkable precision which is
such a feature of this conflation. It will shortly be noted that
section four has in it a similar redaction which contains 745
letters, half a letter less than the number expected if two
columns are filled from the same source as the four final
columns of section three.

In other words, section three has a simple structure. The
first half is filled from J1, the second half from the minor
sources. The calculated contents of the section are 11,651
letters and it contains 11,646 letters.

Section four: 10.19-13.20.

Section four is a mirror image of section three. It begins
with 15 columns filled from the minor sources and ends with
15 columns filled from J1. The first half is thirteen columns
from J2 and two from a redactional source. These have in
them 5,040 letters and 745 letters, a total of 5,785 letters.

The second half of the section starts at 11.55 of the text.
At this point the redactor has more than one consideration
to keep in mind. He put 273 letters of redaction into section
one. If he wants to put a similar amount in the second third

of the text he will have to act soon. He will also have to adjust his text to the presence of the story of the raising of Lazarus. This has just gone in, being set out in splendid detail in 11.1-43. It would be remarkable if no further reference to the miracle were to be made in the following text.

The first point of interest is that 11.55 reads, 'And the Jews' Passover was nigh at hand . . .', while 2.13 reads, 'And the Jews' Passover was at hand . . .'. There can be little doubt that the story of the cleansing of the temple came from this position.

The next item of interest is that 11.55-57 add nothing to the narrative sweep and in total they amount to 273 letters. If the plan is to correct for the omission of the adulterous

FIGURE 6.4

The conflation of the gospel illustrated by a model

SECTION FOUR

TEXT

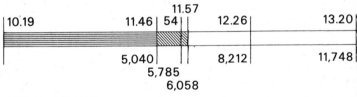

LETTER COUNTS

Number of letters in section   11,748.
Average column   391.6 letters.

TEXT	OLC	EC	ELC	D1	COLC	CELC	D2
10.19-11.46	5,040	13	5,091	−51	5,040	5,091	−51
11.47-54	745	2	783	−38	5,785	5,874	−89
11.55-57	273 ⎫	6	2,350	+77	6,058	8,224	−12
12.1-26	2,154 ⎭				8,212		
12.27-13.28	3,536	9	3,524	+12	11,748		

woman by adding 274 letters to each third of the new version, then this is one place to do it and he is within one letter
of absolute precision.

The redactor then goes on with J1 but he has to insert
references to Lazarus. He does so in three places, at 12.1(b)
'where Lazarus was which had been dead, whom he raised
from the dead', at 12.2(b), 'but Lazarus was one of them that
sat at table with him', and at 12.9-11, where the story of the
plot to kill Lazarus and remove the evidence of the miracle is
recounted.

These three passages contain 36 letters, 38 letters and
222 letters, a total of 296 letters. This is much more than the
redactor can hope to recover in fifteen columns of writing.
He does something to help himself. The fifteen columns contain 5,963 letters, the most densely packed sequence of J1
so far. If we compare it with the expectation of 5,874, we
would conclude that about 89 letters have been pulled back.

The situation at the end of the section would then reflect
the distortion introduced by the insertion of the Lazarus
references. It should have ended at some point after 13.20,
but with the insertions having been made, the redactor has to
prepare for a premature ending to the section. It is therefore
a matter of interest to note that Macgregor questions the
sequence of 13.16-20 and concludes, 'We must either bracket
18-19 as an interpolation by the redactor, added to exclude
Judas from the promise of blessedness, or more probably
transpose 20 to follow 16'. In fact, both alternatives are
correct; 18 and 19 owe their position to the redactor and he
has put them there from some later position in order to end
his section at the right place.

THE THIRD PAIR OF SECTIONS
Sections five and six

Section five: 13.21-18.14, 11.915 letters.

Sections five and six are mirror images. Each starts with
three columns from one source, follows with twenty-four
columns from another source and returns to complete the
section with a final three columns from the initial source.
The large central sequences are useful in confirming the
precise relationship between the J1 and J2 sources.

At the start of section five the redactor has a problem to
deal with which came over from section four. In that section
he had added 296 letters referring to Lazarus and he did
what he could to pull back the excess, by writing 5,963
letters in the second half of the section. If we take the copying from J1 which has been done as a guide, in the first three
sections, forty-five columns had been filled from the J1
source using 17,626 letters. This suggests that the fifteen
columns which end section four would have in them 5,875
letters. So it can be reckoned that having written 5,963
letters he has pulled back 88 letters leaving him with 208 out
of the 296 still to be accommodated.

There is no great complication in doing this. His plan for
the section would seem to be six columns from J1, predicted
contents 9,350 letters, total for the section 11,700. He will
have to write about 208 more, making the contents 11,908,
and to do so will have to write an average of 397 letters per
column instead of 390. Taking a square column of twenty
letters and twenty lines, this means a change of less than
half a letter per line. This will not be difficult to do. But as he
does so he must inevitably spoil the coincidence of columns
and contents of the new book in this section.

He has J1 material at 13.21-35 and 18.1-14. At 13.36-38
he puts in the last component of the correction for the

FIGURE 6.5

The conflation of the gospel illustrated by a model

SECTION FIVE

TEXT

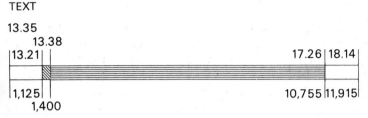

```
13.35
    13.38
 13.21|                                              17.26│18.14│
 1,125|                                            10,755│11,915│
    1,400
```

LETTER COUNTS

Number of letters in section   11,915.
Average column   397.2 letters.

TEXT	OLC	EC	ELC	D1	COLC	CELC	D2
13.21-35	1,125	3	1,191	−66	1,125	1,192	−66
13.36-38	275						
14.1-17.26	9,355	24	9,532	−23	10,755	10,724	+31
18.1-14	1,160	3	1,191	−31	11,915		

adulterous woman. This short passage of Peter's denial is 275 letters. It is a passage taken by Macgregor to be a touchstone of the redactor's motives and interests, and its placing at this point means that each third of the gospel has in it a passage (273 letters in the first, 273 letters in the second and 275 in the third) contributing to a total of 821 letters, almost exactly the content of the *pericope adulterae*. How remarkable a feature this is may be seen by a look at the other gospels. In none is there any group of three paragraphs which exhibits a degree of similarity anything like this.

The section therefore starts with 1,400 letters from J1 and the compensation, 3.52 columns; it goes on with 9,355 letters from J2, 23.55 columns and ends with 2.92 columns from J1. The construction of this section is loose only in comparison with the precision of the other sections. The contents of the section are 11,915 letters, the prediction made from its components was 11,908.

Section six: 18.15-21.25, 11,768 letters.

Having solved his problem in section five the redactor is free to resume his tranquil way. Section six is to be a mirror image of section five and it will have three columns of redaction, twenty-five columns from J1 and finally the last three columns of the gospel filled by redaction. The twenty-four columns of J1 contain 9,404 letters, the predicted contents 9,398 letters. The six columns of redaction have 1,186 and 1,178 letters, a variation of four letters above and below their average. Taking this average to represent the redaction, the predicted contents of the whole section are 11,762 letters, the actual count is 11,768 letters.

The close correspondence of the two redactional passages in this section might suggest a common origin for them and also that theirs is not the origin of the comparable redaction in sections three and four.

The present complex structure of the gospel has been explained by the aggregation of a set of simple principles based on the consistent hypothesis of a conflation. The two major disorders of the text, in chapter 7 and 13, are critical sequences in the conflation and have been ordered to suit the progress of the conflation rather than the logical sequence of the narrative. The one disadvantage of this experimental method is that is makes the creation of the gospel appear so much more complex than it really was. We have to reconstruct the text by calculation and by counting letters. The redactor had documents before him and as he copied from them the relationships which we struggle to recapture were plain before his eyes. We do not know in what format J2 lay before him, but we can see that when he chose to fill, say, fifteen columns of the gospel from J2 he put into these columns what had taken up the comparable space in his source. When he had copied in one third of the fifteen columns of the gospel he could see that he had kept in step by using one third of the J2 with which he planned to fill

FIGURE 6.6

The conflation of the gospel illustrated by a model

SECTION SIX

TEXT

18.15
| 18.27 | 21.14 | 21.25 |

| 1,186 | 10,590 | 11,768 |

LETTER COUNTS

Number of letters in section   11,768.
Average column   392.3 letters.

TEXT	OLC	EC	ELC	D1	COLC	CELC	D2
18.15-27	1,186	3	1,177	+11	1,186	1,177	+11
18.28-21.14	9,404	24	9,412	−8	10,590	10,589	+1
21.15-25	1,178	3	1,177	+1	11,768		

them. He had a straightforward problem of fitting pieces together into a pattern. We follow him by a much more complicated process, but the one advantage which we have is that we can see how incomparably precise were the results of his simple sums.

There is no reason to suppose that we owe the present form of the gospel to more than one mind or hand. The sources of the book are varied, but the production is a unity. If there are many ingredients, there has been only one cook.

The original of the Fourth Gospel

In earlier sections of this book it has been argued that the autograph copy of the *Gospel of John* was written into a codex. Reasons were given for this conclusion, reasons both general and particular. Among the general reasons was that of the leading authority on early Christian manuscripts, C. H. Roberts, who has put on record the fact that no early copy of any New Testament text exists in anything but codex form. Among the particular reasons are the division of the gospel into six sections and the precise arrangements of text within these sections. The divisions demand the regularity provided by a succession of identical pages in contrast to the relative freedom of the roll form. The authors concluded that the gospel was written into a codex though it may well have been something simpler than the surviving examples, most of which come from later periods.

In tracing out the conflation which has produced the present form of the gospel, it became clear that some features of the text offer information about the format of the original. In many cases the information is relative and refers to the proportions of two sources, but there are places where the information is more precise. These notes are simply a gathering of that information and an opinion of its possible interpretation.

The division of the gospel into six sections with an average content of 11,753 letters is more readily understandable as six identical quires in a codex than as six portions of a roll. Six sections of a codex should be identical, six sections of a roll are the same as six small rolls glued together. The remarkable uniformity supports the hypothesis that the book is a codex.

A codex at the end of the first century is likely to have been built up from single sheets folded to make four pages. It is probable that the original of the gospel had a number of pages divisible by four and as it was in six sections the gospel had a number of pages which was some multiple of twenty-four. The average content of a page in the range of practicable sizes is as follows:

No. of pages	Average content of page in letters
120	587.7
144	489.7
168	419.8
192	367.3
216	326.5
240	293.8

The reason for using the anomalous number of 180 columns for the model of the text used in describing the conflation is that the J2 material shows clear signs of a unit of 389.2 letters. In the second section of the gospel, the J2 material is in two parts, one fills eleven columns and the other thirteen columns. Both eleven and thirteen are prime numbers and so represent a fraction not expressed in any other whole numbers unless those made by doubling, trebling or making other multiples of eleven and thirteen. Even doubling the number of columns in the model would mean a column of only 195 letters which is almost without parallel and so is unlikely. J2 therefore was measured in a unit simply related to 389.2 letters. The J1 material and the gospel as a whole can have had any size selected from those listed in the previous table.

The only conjunction of the sizes is where a section of twenty pages will have an average of 587.7 letters per page. This will be almost exactly one and a half units of J1, 1.5 × 389.2 is 583.9 letters. Again there is no lesser conjunction and the only alternatives are columns and pages twice or

thrice this size. Pages twice as large at 1,175 letters are by
no means impossible but would be less frequently found than
are pages of 588 letters. We therefore conclude that the
gospel was written on 120 pages each with an average 588
letters on it. Each section of the gospel would then be twenty
pages written as one quire of five sheets folded to give the
twenty pages.

The layout of a page is a matter of speculation. A page
could have one, two or three columns but this is of little
consequence since a page of 588 letters, say 28 lines of 21
letters, could be split into two columns of 28 lines and 10.5
letters or three columns of 28 lines and 7 letters.

There is one other piece of evidence. At the start of the
conflation the writer must exercise care and this will be
reflected in his counting. A page of 28 lines gives neat divisions into quarters and a line of 21 letters not only gives a
central letter, the eleventh letter of the line, but shows natural
division into three parts. It is to be noted that the prose
insertions into the prologue are 168 letters and 105 letters,
exact multiples of 21 letters and at 8 and 5 lines provide
another unique solution; only lines of 7 letters will also give
whole numbers of lines. This might suggest that while the
book is being written at an average 21 letters per line, the
initial insertions are carefully counted into place. The first
passage of redaction in section three (10.1-18) has 1,491
letters, exactly 71 lines of 21 letters. The next passage
(11.47-54) is half as much, 35 lines and 10 letters.

In the last section of the gospel the conflation of the J2
material has been completed and the two passages provided
by the redactor are 1,186 letters and 1,178 letters. Neither is
a precise multiple of 21 letters; they are 56.5 and 56.1 lines.
But this is just what one expects when three pages which
would hold 1,175 letters have to be filled and are taken as a
single unit.

The prologue of the gospel, without the prose additions is

844 letters, 40 lines of 21 letters plus 4 letters. The omitted *pericope adulterae* is 822 letters, 39 lines and 2 letters.

This led the authors to conclude that the original format of the *Gospel of John* was a codex of one hundred and twenty pages, the average contents of a page being 588 letters, the pages having 28 lines of 21 letters. Naturally such a conclusion can only be an informed opinion but this may well be a case in which one guess is by no means as good as another. This guess fits the evidence better than any of the alternatives. These alternatives represent codices with pages two or three times the size of our choice, perhaps written with two or three columns on each page. There is no evidence which would enable any preference for one or other of these alternatives to be made. Adopting the principle that the simplest explanation of the facts is the best explanation, the codex of one hundred and twenty pages seems best to us.

Chapter Seven

The principles of stylometry

Since the invention of photography, the crime of forgery, once suspected, is almost certain to be proved. The enlargements and comparisons made possible by photography not only enable the writer, or typist, of a text to be identified, they often enable the instrument used in the writing or typing to be identified. What no physical examination of the processes of production or reproduction will reveal is who composed the text or document. To enable the authorship of text to be determined, another science is required, the science of stylometry. The name stylometry is a useful one inasmuch as it correctly describes one of the main purposes of the science, the measurement of those personal aspects of composition which enable the author of a text to be distinguished from any colleague who might have written on the same subject, in the same form, at the same time, for similar reasons and intending a similar readership.

The name stylometry is not useful and indeed can be quite misleading when it is assumed to be a method of translating the literary description of style into mathematical terms. A number of attempts have been made to establish a stylometry of this kind by taking some features noted by literary critics and transposing them into some system of measurement. But no such attempt has produced any generally applicable results.

The history of modern stylometry begins with a letter written in 1851 by Augustus de Morgan, professor of mathematics in London. He wrote to a friend suggesting that the disputed authorship of the Pauline Epistles might be settled by measuring the average length of words used in them. The length of a word was defined as the number of letters in the word.

De Morgan's suggestion is taken as the starting point of modern stylometry as it embodies the three principles now taken as the essentials of stylometry. The first principle is that any particular problem, such as the authorship of the Pauline Epistles, is taken as a specific example of a general problem for which a general solution is required. If you can identify the writer of the Epistles of Paul you can identify the writer of any epistles written in Greek.

The second principle of stylometry was implicit rather than explicit in de Morgan's suggestion. All writers in any language have so much in common with each other, the language itself, the rules and conventions of its use and the social and intellectual assumptions of the times, that they must have much more in common in their writing than they can possibly have peculiar to themselves. The best indicator of a particular author therefore is not the few idiosyncratic habits which he shares with almost none of his fellows, but the different rate at which he uses habits common to all of them. De Morgan understood this and so suggested that all words be included in the examination and not by any literary, grammatical, philological or theological principle of classification but on a characteristic measurable in every word.

The third principle which de Morgan did make quite explicit was that the measurements had to be statistical. No writer ever repeats himself precisely in a text of any size. It is therefore possible to say that in one thousand words of an author you can expect to find an average of fifty occurrences of *AND* but it would be quite nonsensical to say that in any such sample you will find exactly fifty occurrences of *AND*. It is with averages, their calculation, their limitations and their use for comparisons that statistics are concerned.

Briefly, it can be said that, in statistical comparisons as

they are used in stylometry, two texts are taken to be similar if their averages, or other statistics, differ only by an amount which is readily explicable as natural chance variation; they are taken not to be similar if the differences are too large, or too prolonged, to be due to chance variation. Examples shown later will make the principle clear. But the definition of a test of authorship in stylometry is some habit for which the differences within the writings of any author show only chance variation but when compared with the writings of other authors they show larger differences.

It is sad to note that de Morgan's suggestion was of no practical value in the simple form in which he put it forward. The reason is that many of the words in a text reflect the subject of the text rather than the author of the text. The words do contain information about the author but it is swamped by the influence of the subject matter. In the late fifties, Dr. Fucks of Aachen converted word length into a useful test by counting the number of words which separate the equisyllabic words in a text. Starting with words of one syllable, a count is made of how many words come between the successive occurrences of all monosyllabic words, then the count is made for words of two syllables and so on.

The first useful test of authorship should have been due to Udny Yule whose book *The Statistical Study of Literary Vocabulary* was published by Cambridge in 1944. In this book Yule looked at some measures of vocabulary, really showing how complex the subject is rather than solving any problems connected with it. But he also looked at sentence length distributions. He grouped together all sentences having between one and five words, six and ten words and so on. But when he came to the calculations of the measure of variability he forgot that he had grouped his data and so was out by a factor of the square root of five. This led him to conclude that sentence length distributions, in English at any rate, while suggestive, were not a reliable test of authorship.

It fell to Dr. W. C. Wake not only to discover the first scientific test of authorship but to use it to solve the problem for which de Morgan had suggested his test, the authorship of the Pauline corpus. Wake's work began as a doctoral thesis, a summary of which was published as *Sentence Length Distributions of Greek Authors*, in the *Journal of the Royal Statistical Society*, London, 1957. Before looking at any details of Wake's pioneer work it may be useful to see how it conformed to the principles of stylometry. All authors write sentences. This may be only to say that what all authors write is classed as sentences, but sentences are common to all writers of Greek prose. The next point to note is that there is no necessary connection between the length of a sentence and its content. A sentence written on love, war or land-reclamation will be composed of very different words but if each has ten words, they are all ten word sentences. The last point is that sentence length does correspond to a feature of composition. It is often noted that Herodotus writes simple narrative while Thucydides has architectural structure in his sentences.

Wake was interested in the corpus attached to the name of Hippocrates but before he used any test on the corpus he had validated it by an examination over a range of comparable writers of Greek prose. He tested a number of illustrative parallels and it was in doing this that he presented the first scientific solution of the problem of authorship of the Pauline Epistles.

Wake began with a definition of a sentence. For him and all subsequent workers on Greek it is the sequence of words which ends with a full stop, a colon or an interrogation mark. Having adopted this definition, he then showed that if it is used, the differences between editors of texts are so small that they have no effect on the results. He then turned to look at the question of the minimum sample required to represent an author. Wake showed what many people assume, that writers tend to gather long and short sentences in groups so that a sample which is to be fully representative of any author has to be long enough to include all lengths of sentence.

Minimum sample size is determined by three factors. The first is that periodic effect due to the arrangement of sentences by the author, the second is the requirement of statistical theory which suggests that thirty sentences are about the minimum number needed to establish what the pattern of occurrence actually is, the third is the actual instance under examination, since it is the case that while two authors who are very different can be distinguished by using small samples of the statistical minimum size, two authors who closely resemble each other will need much larger samples to separate them.

Wake also had to do a lot of fundamental statistical analysis to discover the patterns to which sentence length distributions conform—what statistics are best used to describe them, and which statistics are independent of each other, so that each test is looking at another aspect of sentence length and not just at the same aspect from another viewpoint.

In the twenty years which have passed since Wake's paper was published, he has been criticised, by scholars who have been careful not to disturb their confident assertions with any evidence, for not dealing with the two points which he had most exhaustively dealt with, namely, the matters of punctuation and of minimum sample size. In two respects Wake's work has been carried further. First, the effect of time on sentence length has been investigated. Though sentence length increases with age, in the two instances examined (see below, footnotes 1 and 2) the effect is so slight

[1] Thomson, N. D., The Chronology of Xenophon, B.Lit. Thesis University of St. Andrews, 1966.

[2] Michaelson, S. and Morton, A. Q., "Things 'Aint' What They Used to Be". In *The Computer in Literary and Linguistic Studies*, ed. A. Jones and R. F. Churchouse, University of Wales, 1976.

that it is difficult to measure for periods of less than twenty years. It is thus not relevant to the problem of the Pauline Epistles or the *Gospel of John*.

The second extension of sentence length studies was to determine in which circumstances it is appropriate not to use the linear scale of sentences grouped 1-5, 6-10, 11-15, 16-20 words, where each group extends by the same amount of five words, but to use a logarithmic scale which might run, 1-5, 6-10, 11-20, 21-40 where each group ends at a point twice the value of the preceding group. Again the choice of scale does not affect the Pauline Epistles.

The foundation having been laid by Wake, further investigations took place to discover tests of authorship independent of sentence length. Such tests are of two kinds, those which use the punctuation of sentences but do not depend on the length of sentence in which the habits are recorded, and those which do not use the punctuation at all.

The first general theory of stylometry was developed for Greek as a result of a series of experiments carried out in Edinburgh University in the early seventies. A set of concordances had been made of a variety of Greek texts and these confirmed what had long been known, if not thought to be of much consequence, that a large part of all Greek texts is made up of repetitions of a few frequent words. What was next shown was a fact not generally acknowledged, that most of these words occurred in a narrow range of positions among the first few words of sentences. The vocabulary of the beginning, middle and end of sentences is quite different. An example of this is given in table 7.1 which shows the vocabulary of first and last words in all the sentences of the *Gospel of John*. The beginning of a sentence is a compact structure. It warns the reader or hearer that something is about to be uttered and that the relation of what is coming to what has been said, or will follow is of a certain kind. The middle of the sentence is a free and flexible structure which

TABLE 7.1

The contrast between the first words and the last words in the sentences of the Gospel of John

Number of occurences of word	Number of words in gospel			
	First words	% of total	Last words	% of total
1	145	12.4	430	36.7
2	33	18.0	82	50.7
3	14	21.6	35	59.7
4	13	26.0	15	64.8
5	6	28.6	9	68.7
6	4	30.7	6	71.7
7	8	35.4	4	74.1
8	2	36.8	7	78.9
9	5	40.7	4	82.0
10	1	41.5		
11	3	44.3	1	82.9
12	3	47.4		
13	5	52.9		
14	2	55.3	2	85.3
15				
16	2	58.1	1	86.7
19			1	88.3
20	2	65.5		
24	1	63.5	1	90.3
26	1	65.8		
27	1	68.1		
28	1	70.5		
30	1	73.0		
32			1	93.1
39			1	96.4
42			1	100.0
55	1	77.7		
70	1	83.8		
71	1	89.8		
120	1	100.0		
	257		601	

The percentages are cumulative. For example, 58.1% of first words and 86.7% of last words occur 16 times or fewer.

has a mixed vocabulary; in the middle of the sentence are found both frequent and rare words. The end of the sentence is another compact structure, consisting of the preparation for the last word and the choice of last word. In the last position frequent words are rarely found although this does not mean that some words occupy the last position fairly often. These words which have a marked preference for the final position are not very frequent when the count is made of all words in all positions.

Upon this foundation was erected a theory of word movement and word mobility. Some words were found to occur frequently in a narrow range of positions and almost never outside this range. Other words moved freely in sentences and are found in all positions from the first word to the last, although many such words stop short of complete mobility and avoid the actual first or last position. Many words show a marked preference for some positions near to the start or finish of sentences but also occur in a range of other positions. Schoolchildren are taught not to finish a sentence with a preposition, but one can write and say that the one word never found as the last word of a sentence is word, w. In stating the rule, you have broken it.

Words which move freely reflect or illuminate the sentence length distributions. The comparison may be carried a little further with profit. If you stand some distance from a large building and shine a spotlight on it, you will see a small part of the edifice at any moment but if you keep a trace of the moving beam this will reveal the outline of the whole. Thus a record of the positions in which a fully mobile word occurs will trace out the main features of the sentence length distribution of the sentences in which the occurrences have been recorded.

But many mobile words do not occur in all kinds of sentences. For example, imperatives usually occur in short commands. This means that particular aspects of sentences can be picked out for separate examination. This process is rather like looking at a group of coloured objects through a set of colour filters. If you look through a red filter, all red objects appear grey or black or are invisible. Other colours will be altered. In exactly this way the movement of certain words can be used to look at selected groups of sentences. In the paper in which the theory was described two examples are given. The first is from the dialogues of Plato. These are intractable material for the student of sentence length distributions because they are a mixture of dialogue exchange in very short sentences and continuous prose with the normal range of sentences. Samples reflect the mixture of prose and dialogue more than they reflect anything else. The difficulty can be avoided by excluding all sentences with five words or fewer but if this is done then two objections are offered. The first is that a particular stratagem has been used to get round a particular difficulty and it has been done by the experimenter and not by the author of the text. But if you record the positional distributions of the conjunction *kai*, this traces the outline of the sentences in which it occurs and, as it does not occur very often in the short sentences which cause the difficulty, these simply vanish from the record. The presence or absence of dialogue ceases to be a problem. This has been accomplished using a rule of general application which operates on the material as written by Plato and not as selected by the experimenter.

The second example is taken from the other end of the scale by selecting a word which usually occurs in the longer and more elaborate sentences. One such word is the epithet *Christos*. In *I Corinthians* Paul uses this word in sentences which average 20.6 words, not quite twice as long as the average for all the sentences in the epistle which is 12.1 words. The writer of *Ephesians* uses *Christos* in sentences which average 61.1 words, more than twice the length of his average of 30.3 words.

A set of tests of authorship which are independent of sentence length is based upon the occurrence of a group of words, mainly particles, which show a strong tendency to occur in a few positions, most often among the first few words of sentences. The tests can be made either by recording the proportion of the sentences in the text which have the count word in the preferred position, or by recording the proportion of occurrences of the count word which stand in the preferred position.

One advantage of having a general theory of stylometry is that it is a simple matter to make a list of the words in a text which can prove useful as tests of authorship. The list having been compiled, it is equally simple to use it for comparisons between the texts under examination.

There are circumstances in which it might be unwise to accept the punctuation of a text. In such circumstances there are two alternative procedures which can be followed. The first is to use the occurrence of one frequent word as a marker and record the occurrence of other frequent words in the intervals between successive occurrences of the mark-word. For example, you can count the occurrences of the particle *de* between occurrences of the conjunction *kai*. A paper describing a full set of such tests has been in print for some time.[3] These are later applied to the text of the gospel, though not because the punctuation is regarded as suspect.

The second resource is to count the occurrence of proportional pairs of words. These are simply pairs of words which have been found to occur in consistent proportion within the writing of an author. No other significance should be attached to the coupling for although in some cases it may be easy to suggest a connection between the two members of the pair there are equally attested pairs where any such suggestion would be incredible. The first pair to

[3] *The Spaces in Between*, S. Michaelson and A. Q. Morton, *Lasla Review* 1, 1972.

come to light was the combination of the two most frequent Greek adjectives *pas* and *polus*. About 2% of a Greek text is made up of the repetition of adjectives but, when samples were taken of the size likely to prove useful in New Testament studies, the occurrences of all other adjectives were swamped by the occurrences of these two frequent words. Comparisons of adjectives boiled down to the comparison of the proportion of these two words. This test is used in the examination of the gospel as are two others, the occurrences of the different forms of the negative particle *ou*, *ouk* or *oux* and the occurrence of the genitive forms of the third person pronoun.

Great advantages accrued from having a general theory to apply. One has already been noted, namely, that it is possible to make a list of all the tests which will be relevant to any particular comparison. Another advantage is that a particular test which it might be difficult to validate in an isolated comparison can be readily validated by similar comparisons.

As an example of this situation, the particle *oun* is not frequently used by most Greek writers, at least not at the rate at which it occurs in parts of the Gospel of John. If a test of authorship is to be based upon the occurrence of *oun*, then it would be difficult to find a number of texts and authors sufficient to validate the test. But as soon as the particular case is put as a general principle, that all words which behave in this way are suitable for use in tests of authorship, validation becomes a matter of simple routine.

Before going on to the application of stylometric tests to the gospel and its principal components, it may be useful to illustrate the contrast between the traditional stylometry, the simple counting of features thought to be, or assumed to be, relevant to a determination of authorship, and the modern science of stylometry. The illustration is based upon vocabulary, which is still, to most students of literature, the most striking aspect of composition.

One of the authors was presented with a challenge in the following pattern. The owner of the copyright of Sherlock Holmes invited two young men to write some new adventures for the great detective. One of the writers, Nicholas Utechin, has long been connected with the Sherlock Holmes Society and has a reputation as an imitator of the master. With his colleague he wrote a new adventure, *The Earthquake Machine*. The two men wrote blocks of the book, each taking several chapters at a time so that the finished book is a sandwich of two styles. All that was known to the experimenter at the start of the investigation was that the book had been written in this way, and which chapters were written by A and which by B. The first question was, Can the two writers A and B be separated from Holmes, i.e. Conan Doyle, and from each other? A supplementary question arose when Utechin published an article in a literary monthly on French villages, Can this be used to prove he is A or B?

Computer concordances were prepared of samples from two Sherlock Holmes stories and from the different sections of *The Earthquake Machine*. Reading through these concordances it was at once obvious that some words occurred in A and not in B, and vice versa, words not directly connected with the subject of the writing. It was decided to make two lists, the words which occur in A and not in B, and vice versa, subject only to the conditions that the words should not be relevant to the subject matter and should occur at least five times in the sample.

So in list A we have eleven words which occur more than fifty-five times in sample A and not at all in sample B. List B has three words occurring more than fifteen times in sample B and not at all in sample A. No one would suggest that words in either list would not be used by the writer of the other list if the circumstances were appropriate, but what it would seem very reasonable to suggest is that if we got a sample written by either A or B we could count the occurrences of these words and should find a simple majority of occurrences which would decide the question. Of the words in the A list, Utechin's article has twenty-three occurrences, just over two occurrences per word. Of words in the B list it has eight occurrences, just over two per word. Further experiments soon revealed that this technique of choosing vocabulary items, assumed to record some preference of the

Sherlock Holmes Word Lists.

A (Not in B)	*B* (Not in A)
every	away
few	because
forward	replied
morning	
nothing	
outside	
own (possessive adjective)	
surely	
these	
through	
told	

writer, could produce either a positive match for the right author, or a positive match for the wrong author, or, as in this example, a completely non-committal balance.

Vocabulary is a much more complex phenomenon than most students of literature realise. Not only is the choice of word conditioned by the subject matter and the writer's relationships to the subject and to his readers, it is also constrained by the historical situation in which he writes, by his social milieu and by reasons which make excellent literary sense but are certain disorder for statistics. When a writer has written 'boats' or 'ships' a number of times he will change and use 'craft' or 'vessels' for variety. But as soon as it is realised that a choice of word in one page has been determined by what was, or was not, written on another page, the basis of simple statistics has gone. No doubt the presence or absence of certain words, be the presence or absence absolute or only relative, does indicate authorship, but it can also arise from many other causes and in simple analyses it can be completely misleading. The only safe procedure is to leave the rare words and look at those which occur in all subjects and in all circumstances. These are the frequent words, the filler words, the connectives and particles. They have the great advantage of being habitual in use by reason of their frequency and of the habits being so established as to be almost entirely unconscious. So little is the role of the frequent words appreciated that many scholars are still re-sisting any claim that one can determine the authorship of a text by looking at them. Yet the problem just mentioned, the separation of Sherlock Holmes from his two imitators, and the demonstration that one of them changed his own habits so little even when writing the imitation that he can be identi-fied from his free composition, can be solved by looking at no more than two of the most frequent words in English, the definite article *THE* and the indefinite article *A* or *AN*.

In the experiment there were four samples. Each had been tested for internal consistency. Two samples known as A and B were from the two men who had imitated Holmes. The third sample was from two of Conan Doyle's stories and the fourth sample came from an article written by one of the imitators, Nicholas Utechin. Inspection of the entries for *THE* gave the results shown on page 92.

Stylometry as a science has now been recognised by the courts and has been used to show that a confession attributed to an accused has been fabricated.

The basic principle of stylometry is simple and can be readily illustrated. Suppose that two texts each have two hundred sentences. In text A, forty of the sentences have the conjunction *KAI* as their first word. In text B, sixty of the

Number of occurrences of	A	B	Holmes	Utechin
THE	210	180	350	316
pb OF, %	18.1	11.0	10.3	15.2
pb ON, %	1.9	9.4	4.0	1.3
Number of occurrences of TO	62	55	188	101
fb THE, %	27.4	7.3	11.1	31.7

pb means preceded by, fb is followed by.
OF THE separates Holmes from A and Utechin.
ON THE separates B from A, from Holmes and Utechin.
TO THE separates B, and Holmes, from A and Utechin.
Therefore B is not A nor is it Holmes.
Utechin is either A or B; he is not B, therefore A is Utechin.

sentences start with *KAI*. The question is whether or not these two texts show a consistent habit. This question can never be answered by simple comparisons. One critic will argue that the two texts certainly differ, after all in one of them the rate of using *KAI* as the first word of sentences is no less than 50% more than it is in the other. To this a colleague will reply that while one hundred and forty sentences in one text do not have *KAI* as their first word, one hundred and sixty sentences in the other do not have it and the difference is only ten sentences above and below the average of one hundred and fifty sentences with words other than *KAI* as their first word.

It is to resolve such problems that statistics have been developed. The starting point is to make a mathematical model of the situation. Suppose we take two lots of two hundred cards and on some we write *KAI* to denote a sentence having the conjunction as its first word. We begin with forty such cards in the first set and sixty in the second. If we put the cards together we have one set of four hundred cards with one hundred *KAI* cards in the set. If we then shuffle the cards and deal out sets of two hundred we would expect to find in a set about fifty *KAI* cards. We would not expect to find exactly fifty cards very often, but we would expect to find numbers of cards near to fifty quite often and numbers much above or below fifty rather less often. But all that can be said with complete certainty is that there cannot be less than no card with *KAI*, or more than one hundred such cards. The number in between can be ranged as occurring more or less often by keeping a record of the results of a large number of shufflings and dealings.

If the difference between two lots of cards is one which would occur quite often by natural chance variation, such as is the result of shuffling and dealing cards, then for such a difference no other explanation need be given or indeed can be given. If the difference is large and chance would be unlikely to have produced it, then some other explanation for the difference must be sought. If the two texts are by the same author then the explanation would be that his habit had changed from one text to the other and so could not be regarded as consistent.

Stylometry is based upon those habits which are consistent within the works of all writers of the class under examination, writers of English verse or of Greek prose. To be useful these habits should not only be consistent within the works of any writer but differ from one writer to another. In practice the only difficulties arise when works in contrasting literary forms have to be compared. When poetry has to be compared with prose, or dialogue with continuous narrative, many habits change in sympathy. If material is plentiful there will be few problems for the habits which are stable, even with the maximum contrast in literary form, since those vary little from writer to writer and so large samples will prove reliable and effective. But if the material is limited and the only samples are in different literary forms, care must be exercised to prevent any difference due to the contrast in forms being interpreted as a difference due to multiple authorship.

Stylometry is now so far advanced that the only real problems are those which concern texts which have been revised or re-written. It is usually not too difficult to tell when this has been done, but to come to any further conclusions can be very difficult indeed.

Chapter Eight

The application of stylometry to the text of the Gospel

Stylometry is a comparative subject and must start with an axiomatic assumption that some piece of text is by the author, say, Paul or John. It may seem to some scholars a crude way to begin an enquiry but this pattern of argument and investigation is not without merit. It reminds the scholar that some such assumption has to be made at some point and the real choice lies between making a conscious assumption and keeping it under constant review or never making explicit what assumption has been made. If a text is not homogeneous then the matter of initial definition becomes quite crucial. For example, the central section of Plato's *Seventh Epistle* differs from the start and finish. If a scholar makes his decision early or late, he will choose Plato as the author; if he makes up his mind in the middle he will decide against Plato. Both are right and both are wrong. The correct conclusion is that parts are by Plato and other parts are not.

Another advantage which follows from the statistical nature of the argument is that the decision will be made on quantifiable evidence. If one piece of evidence suggests that the nominal author is unlikely to have written the text and gives odds of a million to one against his having done so, this far outweighs a dozen reasons which suggest the odds are about even money that he did or did not write it.

There can be no doubt that Johannine studies would be much simpler if every student who has advanced a theory of the gospels or the epistles had stated what initial assumptions he had made, upon which sections of the text he had based his assumptions, and what evidence he adduced to justify having done so.

In this book the primary assumption is that the author of the *First Epistle of John* is one person who can be called Jay. The reasons for starting with the epistle are of two kinds. The first would be the literary and historical reasons for regarding First John not as a letter written to a person or group or to some place, but as a general homily similar in many respects to material in the gospel, particularly in some of the sections we label J2. It is these similarities which have led to the common argument that First John has an intimate connection with the gospel. On the other hand there are passages in the gospel which preclude any simple correspondence of the authorship of First John and the composition of the gospel.

The second set of reasons for starting with First John are given in the following tables but these can be simply summarised. First John is, as far as present stylometric techniques can tell, a homogeneous text and so is suitable for use as a touchstone. As can be seen from the first of the tables, First John has in it one hundred and forty-four sentences and this is enough to supply three samples for comparisons within the epistle. In all the tests which can be applied, the epistle is a unity. This means that it can be used as a single sample of one hundred and forty-four sentences.

The next step is to compare First John with the six J2 sections in turn. It is not enough just to make the comparisons, for First John is a homily without a historical foundation in the sense that some of the homilies within the gospel are connected with some historical incident, for example, the feeding of the multitude or the raising of Lazarus. If a foundation of this kind were thought to be essential for a passage in the gospel, presumably it would have to be supplied and so it is necessary not only to enquire whether any stylometric differences exist between First John and the J2 sections but also to discover if any statistically significant differences which may be found arise from the J2 section as a whole or merely from some part of it. In these comparisons sections two and three of J2 are so short that it would be difficult either to make distinctions within them or to distinguish them from other sources which are also as short.

A logical sequence of testing the epistle and gospel begins with the integrity of the epistle and with its sentence length distributions. These are set out in table 8.1 The calculation of Davie's coefficient indicates that a logarithmic scale is appropriate and from the table it can be seen that the epistle as a whole does fit a log normal distribution based upon the

TABLE 8.1

The First Epistle of John

A. The sentence length distributions (Linear scale)

Number of words in sentence	Number of sentences in First John			
	1-48	49-96	97-144	Total
1-5	—	5	2	7
6-10	18	9	6	33
11-15	13	20	15	48
16-20	10	7	14	31
21-25	3	3	8	14
26-30	3	3	3	9
31-35	—	1	—	1
56-60	1	—	—	1
Totals	48	48	48	144
Log. mean	1.085	1.090	1.165	1.113
Log. standard error	.036	.020	.029	

Table 8.1—(*continued*)

B. The whole epistle (log scale)

Number of words in sentence	Number of such sentences in	
	First John	Log. normal distribution
1-5	7 ⎱ 19	4.8 ⎱ 16.0
6-7	12 ⎰	11.2 ⎰
8-9	15	17.1
10-11	12	19.2
12-13	25	18.6
14-15	17	16.0
16-17	11	13.8
18-19	11	10.7
20-21	13	8.1
22-25	10	10.8
26-30	9 ⎱ 11	7.3 ⎱ 13.8
31 or more	2 ⎰	6.5 ⎰
Totals	144	144.1

Chi squared for the comparison is 7.02 for seven degrees of freedom.

C. A comparison of the gospel and a log normal distribution

Number or words in sentence	Number of such sentences in	
	Gospel	Log. normal distribution
1-5	99	134.6
6-10	384	340.8
11-15	318	313.8
16-20	197	193.2
21-25	100	99.5
26-30	37	46.8
31-35	23	23.4
36 or more	13	18.7
Totals	1171	1170.8

Chi squared is 21.22 for five degrees of freedom.
For the cell 1-5 words it is 12.44.
For the cell 6-10 words 5.35.

observed median and first and third quartiles. When the epistle is divided into three parts of forty-eight successive sentences, no significant difference is found between any one of them and the others or the rest of the epistle.

TABLE 8.2

The occurrence of the conjunction kai *in I John*

A. The distribution of *kai* in sentences

Number of occurrences of *kai* in sentence	Number of such sentences in First John			
	1-48	49-96	97-144	Total
0	19	19	21	59
1	16	18	19	53
2	11	10	7	28
3	1	1	1	3
9	1	—	—	1
Totals	48	48	48	144
Mean number of occurrences	1.04	0.85	0.75	0.88
Standard error	—	—	—	.09

B. The occurrence of *kai* as the first word of sentences

Number of sentences with *kai* as first word	Number of sentences in sequence
6	25
4	25
7	25
6	25
6	25
4	19
Totals 33	144

Table 8.2—(*continued*)

C. The positional distribution of the occurrence of the conjunction
kai in the epistle

Number of occurrences	Forward distribution		Backward distribution	
	Mean	Standard error	Mean	Standard error
132	0.887	.029	0.959	.022

The difference is not statistically significant.

TABLE 8.3

The comparison of the First Epistle of John with the Gospel of John

A. Feature

	Number in gospel observed	Number in epistle observed	Number expected
Number of sentences	1171	144	144
KB	557	85	70.3
K1	120	33	16.8
D2	179	5	19.6
G2	43	3	4.7
E1	59	11	6.5
O2	189	—	20.7

K1 and E1 denote sentences with *kai* and *ean* as their first word.

D2, G2, O2 denote sentences with *de*, *gar*, and *oun* as their second word.

KB denotes a sentence with one or more occurrences of *kai*. The expectations are in the proportion of the sentences in the epistle, 144 to the sentences in gospel and epistle, 1,315 multiplied by the number of occurrences of the feature in gospel and epistle.

The differences in proportion of K1, D2 and O2 are statistically significant.

The sentence length distribution of the gospel is anomalous. In no other piece of Greek prose is there any comparable record of a distribution with such a wide flat top to it. There are sixty-seven sentences with six words in them, fifty-nine with fifteen words, and the modal value, with eighty-five sentences, is nine words. This strongly suggests a combination of distributions, and occurrence only to be expected if the book is a compilation from different sources. At this stage all that need be recorded is that the epistle appears to be homogeneous and its sentence length distribution fits a log normal distribution, while the gospel is

TABLE 8.4

The sentence length distributions of the J2 sequences and First John

Number of words in sentence	Number of such sentences in							Epistle First John
	1	2	3	4	5	6	Total	
1-5	8	—	1	16	7	9	41	7
6-10	28	12	9	27	28	58	162	33
11-15	27	13	10	18	24	48	140	48
16-20	21	9	13	12	14	23	92	31
21-25	10	5	4	5	6	11	41	14
26-30	4	3	3	—	2	5	17	9
31-35	1	2	2	2	2	3	12	1
36-40	1	—	2	—	1	2	6	—
41-45	—	—	—	—	—	1	1	—
56-60	—	—	—	—	—	—	—	1
Totals	100	44	44	80	84	160	512	144
og. mean	1.087	1.138	1.176	0.968	1.051	1.106	1.067	1.113
og. standard error mean	0.026	0.034	0.031	0.034	0.027	0.019	0.012	0.018

TABLE 8.5

A comparison of the sentence length distributions of First John and the J2 sequences in the gospel

| Number of words in sentence | Number of such sentences in | | | |
| | J2 | | First John | |
	Observed	Expected	Observed	Expected
1-5	41	37.4	7	10.5
6-10	162	152.1	33	42.8
11-15	140	146.9	48	41.3
16-20	92	96.3	31	27.1
21-25	41	43.0	14	12.1
26-30	17 ⎫	36.9	9 ⎫	10.4
31 or more	19 ⎭		2 ⎭	
Totals	512	512.6	144	144.2

Chi squared is 7.70, for five degrees of freedom.

heterogeneous and its sentence length distribution does not fit a log normal distribution.

The most frequent word in the epistle, and the gospel, is the conjunction *kai* and the next set of tables shows the main features of the occurrence of *kai* in the sentences of the epistle. The conclusion to be drawn from them is that there is no evidence which would cast doubt upon the integrity of the epistle. The last table is a simple comparison which shows that the gospel cannot be taken as a unity in comparison with the epistle. The rate of occurrence of the other particles and connectives in the epistle do not allow for much testing of the integrity of the epistle and for that reason they are left for later consideration and comparison.

The logical sequence of testing in the gospel is to start with the First Epistle, which has turned out to be homogeneous in every test, compare the epistle with the sequences of J2 and then compare both the epistle and the J2 sequences with the J1 sequences. One reason for doing this has already been given. There is a close relation between the epistle and parts of the gospel. If the conflation theory is correct, the connection is more likely to be between the additions to the composite text than with the underlying composite text. The situation may be that passages have been added to a document which is about as complex as the *Gospel of Mark* and so it is not likely that the additions will have the range and variety of sources of the foundation document.

TABLE 8.6

The sentence length distributions of the J1 sequences in the gospel

Number of words in sentence	Number of such sentences in J1						
	S_1	S_2	S_3	S_4	S_5	S_6	S_7
1-5	14	2	—	12	1	9	20
6-10	20	5	5	62	10	36	81
11-15	26	12	7	44	6	31	55
16-20	14	—	6	26	4	24	26
21-25	13	3	4	10	3	9	22
26-30	—	—	—	3	—	8	7
31-35	2	—	—	1	—	3	4
36-40	—	—	—	—	1	1	1
41-45	1	—	—	—	—	—	—
46-50	—	—	—	—	—	1	—
51-55	—	—	—	—	—	—	—
56-60	1	—	—	—	—	—	—
Totals	91	25	22	158	25	122	216
Log. mean	1.032	—	—	1.021	—	1.089	1.029
Log. standard error of mean	0.031	—	—	0.019	—	0.024	0.018

TABLE 8.7A

The occurrence of the conjunction kai in the sentences of First John and the J2 sequences of the gospel

Number of occurrences of kai in sentence	Number of such sentences in							
	S_1	S_2	S_3	S_4	S_5	S_6	S_{1-6}	First John
0	54	18	20	42	48	83	265	56
1	31	22	20	21	26	53	173	54
2	10	4	4	15	7	12	52	30
3	5	—	—	2	3	6	16	3
4	—	—	—	—	—	6	6	—
9	—	—	—	—	—	—	—	1
Totals	100	44	44	80	84	160	512	144
Log. mean	0.66	0.68	0.64	0.71	0.58	0.74	0.68	0.92
Log. standard error of mean							0.04	0.09

TABLE 8.7B

The comparison of the epistle and the J2 sequences with the expected values of a negative binomial distribution having the same mean and variance

	Number of such sentences in			
	First John		J2 sequences	
Number of occurrences of *kai* in sentence	Observed	Expected	Observed	Expected
0	56	62.9	265	268.3
1	54	47.1	173	167.4
2	30 ⎫		52	59.4
3 or more	4 ⎬	34.0	22	16.9
Totals	144	144.0	512	512.0
	Chi squared is 1.77 for one degree of freedom.		Chi squared is 2.67 for one degree of freedom.	

The sequence of testing is also logical. It starts with the sentence length distributions, goes on to those tests which are based upon sentence length and are not independent of it, then to those tests which are independent of sentence length but use the punctuation of the text, and finally to the tests which are not only independent of sentence length but make no use of the punctuation of the text.

The results of the tests are displayed in the series of tables set out in this chapter but the results can be summarised in this way. The First Epistle of John is homogeneous in every test applied to it. The sequences of J2 closely resemble each other and the epistle, but in many of the tests one of the sequences will show a statistically significant difference from the others. The cause of the difference is often localised so that it reflects a feature of some part of the sequence rather than the whole sequence. It is therefore not possible to argue that the writer of First John is also the writer of the J2 sequences, but it would be entirely reasonable to suggest that there is some close connection between them. If the sequences had been adapted for use in the gospel either by a redactor not the writer of First John, or even by the writer of First John, then the necessary changes could well explain the close resemblance and the few but clear differences.

In contrast to this, the J1 passages differ very markedly from each other and from the J2–First John material. The second and third sequences are so short that little useful information emerges from an examination of them. The fourth and sixth sequences show no difference from each other but in almost every test the first sequence, the fourth and sixth together and the final seventh sequence differ from each other and from J2–First John. The tables include some notes on the site of particular differences and these will surprise no student of the gospel.

From the examination three conclusions are to be drawn. The first is that the epistle is a homogeneous document. The second is that the J1 sequences are diverse and show large differences within them, and between them and the remainder of the gospel, but the J2 sequences show minor differences within themselves. The different nature of the two components of the gospel shows in many tests and for this some explanation such as a difference of origin is required. The third conclusion is that the writer of the epistle is not the writer of the J2 passages as they now stand though some connection with these passages would be a reasonable explanation of the resemblances between the epistle and the J2 material.

The tables also show the limitations of this analysis. For short sequences, with just over twenty sentences or as many

TABLE 8.8

The occurrence of the conjunction kai *in the J1 sequences of the gospel*

Number of occurrences of *kai* in sentence	Number of such sentences in			
	S_1	S_4	S_6	S_7
0	37	95	66	116
			35	56
1	29	45	18	31
				6
2	19	18	2	7
			1	
3	3	—	—	—
4	2	—	—	—
9	1	—	—	—
Totals	91	158	122	216
Mean	1.02	0.51	0.69	0.76
Standard error of mean	0.14	0.06	0.09	0.07

TABLE 8.9

*The occurrence of some words in preferred positions
at the start of sentences in the First Epistle of John
and the J2 sequences in the gospel*

Word	Preferred position	Occurrences in					In preferred position First John
		S_1	S_4	S_5	S_6	Total	
Kai	First	8	10	5	17	40	33
De	Second or Third	12	9	19	18	58	5
Oun	Second	10	15	17	2	44	—
	Totals	100	80	84	160	424	144

occurrences of the conjunction *kai*, differences would appear
only if they were extreme and so would rarely be encoun-
tered. This is true but is should not be assumed that this also
means that a section of this size can be introduced into a
text without hope of detection. What it does mean is that, to
show up clearly, such a section would have to be a marked
contrast to its context.

The results of the stylometric examination are largely
negative but they are no less useful for being so. To know
that a particular proposition is not tenable is to go some way
towards discovering one that is.

1. *The sentence length distributions*

The comparison of the sentence length distributions of the
six J2 sequences shows that there is a statistically significant
difference which involves the third and fourth sequences. If
one or other is extracted from the set, the difference vanishes.
That it is sequence four which is anomalous is shown by an

inspection of the data. The reason for the difference is the presence in sequence four of sixteen sentences having five words or fewer. Sequence five, with much the same number of sentences in it as sequence four, has only seven such sentences and sequence six, which has twice as many sentences as either sequence four or five, has nine such sentences. That this is the anomalous sequence is confirmed by making a chart of the order statistics of the means of the six sequences.

The sentence length distribution of First John is a reasonable fit to a log normal distribution. The sentence length

TABLE 8.10

The occurrence of some frequent words in preferred positions in the components of the Gospel of John

1. The J1 sequences

Word	Preferred position	S_1	S_2	S_3	S_4	S_5	S_6	S_7
Kai	W1	21	2	4	14	2	7	24
De	W2 or W3	11	6	8	26	3	18	42
Oun	W2	3	6	7	30	1	25	64
Gar	W2 or W3	—	1	—	8	—	5	3
Number of sentences in sample		91	25	22	158	25	122	216

2. The J2 sequences

Word	Preferred position	S_1	S_4	S_5	S_6	Total	First John
Kai	W1	8	10	5	17	40	33
De	W2 or W3	12	9	19	18	58	5
Oun	W2	10	15	17	2	44	—
Number of sentences in sample		100	80	84	160	424	144

TABLE 8.11

*The significant differences between parts of J1
and J2 in the occurrence of some frequent words
recorded in the intervals between successive
occurrences of the conjunction* kai

Count word	Number of occurrences	Section of J1			First John
		S_1	S_4	S_6	
Alla	0	88	68	64	122
	1 or more	4	16	16	9
Gar	0	92	77	71	128
	1 or more	—	7	9	3
De	0	82	65	59	122
	1 or more	10	19	21	9
Me	0	92	73	67	117
	1 or more	—	11	13	14
Ou	0	78	63	51	100
	1 or more	14	21	29	31

		Section of J2		First John
		S_1	S_6	
Gar	0	53	114	128
	1 or more	12	4	3
Oun	0	57	115	131
	1 or more	8	3	—

distribution of all six sequences taken together is not a good
fit to a log normal distribution although Davie's coefficient
suggests that the log scale is the appropriate one. The
sequences have too few short sentences, sentences with five
words or fewer, forty-one against an expected fifty-eight, and
too many sentences with six to ten words, one hundred and
sixty-two against an expected one hundred and forty. The

most likely reason for this is that the distribution is not log normal, it has too few short sentences with five words or fewer but this difference is not statistically significant unless the samples contain a few hundred sentences. There is an exact parallel in Aristotle who writes what can be taken as a log normal distribution above five words but has a deficiency of sentences with fewer than five words, a deficiency which is only statistically significant with samples of five hundred sentences or more. If First John is a parallel instance, the difference between the observed distribution and a log normal distribution with the same constants would not show in a sample of one hundred and forty-four sentences. That this is likely to be the case is shown by taking the sentence length distribution as a contingency table; in this there is no statistically significant difference between the sequences and the epistle.

All that really requires an explanation is the large number of sentences in sequence four having five words or fewer. Of the sixteen such sentences, six are questions and four are sentences which immediately follow an interrogation mark. The sentences are all direct speech. The following sequence having four more sentences in it, has seven sentences of five words or fewer and of the seven only two are questions and one follows an interrogation mark. The difference between the two sequences lies in the proportion of direct speech and dialogue exchange and so the statistically significant difference between sequence four and the others can be attributed to this cause. Confirmation will come later when tests not affected by dialogue or direct speech are employed.

2. *The occurrence of the conjunction* kai

The most frequent word in both gospel and epistle is the conjunction *kai*. As one might expect in a homogeneous text the occurrence of *kai* in the sentences of First John fits a negative binomial distribution. But the comparison of the epistle with the J2 sequences reveals statistically significant differences between them. In the epistle, sentences with no occurrence of *kai* and sentences having one occurrence are about as common, fifty-six against fifty-four. But in the J2 sequences there are two hundred and sixty-five sentences with no occurrence of *kai* and only one hundred and seventy-three with one occurrence. This difference might well arise from the cause noted earlier, the presence of direct speech and the short sentences in which it is presented. There is no difference between any of the J2 sequences and the remainder of them, but when the comparison is made of the expectations based upon the occurrence in the epistle, then all the J2 sequences have relatively too many sentences with no occurrence of *kai* in them.

There is another statistically significant difference; it concerns the sentences which have two occurrences of *kai* in them. Sequence four has too many such sentences yet it alone of the six sequences matches the epistle in this characteristic.

The First Epistle of John and the J2 sequences resemble each other but are by no means identical. The differences might be explained by the difference in form, particularly the presence of direct speech and of interrogation in some parts of the J2 sequences. Later tests will confirm or reject this hypothesis.

The writer of First John has a marked habit of using the conjunction *kai* to introduce a sentence; thirty-three of the one hundred and forty-four sentences in the epistle begin with this word. If the epistle is taken in six successive samples, the maximum number which will preserve the expectation of five occurrences per sample, the whole epistle is consistent in this habit. A test of the four J2 sequences large enough to compare with the epistle, reveals no difference between the sequences but a very large difference between the sequences and the epistle. In the sequences, 9% of the sentences have *kai* as their first word, in the epistle, three times as many, 22.9%.

3. *Other words in preferred positions*

In the habit of using the particle *de* as the second or third word of sentences, sequence five shows a statistically significant difference from the others. The seat of the difference is clearly to be seen in the story of Lazarus, chapter 11 verses 1–13. Here a succession of fifteen sentences has no fewer than seven with *de* as their second word. The rest of the sequence has twelve such sentences out of sixty-nine. Again there is a large difference between the sequences taken together and the epistle; 3.5% of the sentences of the epistle have *de* as their second word, 13.7% of the sentences in the sequence.

The occurrence of the particle *oun* shows a similar pattern to that of *de*; one sequence, this time sequence six, differs from the other sequences but not from the epistle.

Finally there falls to be recorded one of the most striking regularities of them all. It came to light only after the analysis of the gospel was complete. The number of letters in First John is 9,508; Second John has 1,132 and Third John 1,118; the total for all three is 11,758, five letters more than the average for sections 2, 4 and 6 of the gospel. First John compares with the largest sequence of J1, the central sequence of section six, which has in it 9,404 letters. It is difficult to escape the implication that gospel and epistles were designed on the same principles.

Chapter Nine

The conflation and its effects

The thesis we have advanced is that the Fourth Gospel is not a homogeneous composition but a conflation of sources used by a compiler to make a new book. This is not a staggering suggestion since the same is known to be true of all other major books of the New Testament, the Synoptic Gospels, *Acts* and *Revelation*. The compiler therefore had to take decisions about the size of book he intended to make, what material he was to use and how he was to order it. He also had to decide at various junctures how he was to link the disparate units of which his book was to be compounded. Some of these decisions had to be taken at the outset, others at the point when they arose. Since his book is of columns and pages of a regular size this is the obvious unit of measurement and his main sources would be assessed in these terms in relation to the new book.

In general outline his book will be a gospel in the sense that it will recount events in the life of Jesus from the beginning in Galilee to the trial, crucifixion and resurrection. This is the plan of his major source which we have called J1. It is parallel to but not identical with the *Gospel of Mark* which was used for the same purpose by Matthew and Luke. But whereas their additional material consisted of more Galilean or extra-Judean traditions and public teaching, his will include new extra-Galilean incidents together with private instruction given by Jesus to his disciples. Of this new material, which we have designated J2, the synoptic authors know nothing. His task therefore is to insert or enclose this new material within the major source and encompass all within a codex of one hundred and twenty pages, so making

114

a new book, the Fourth Gospel. So long as he is careful to see that any rearrangement or substitutions he makes in the use of his sources do not disturb the length of the contribution they make to the new book, he will preserve the freedom he needs to fit his material to size.

The sources keep pace exactly for the first two-thirds of the book. At page 80 he has filled forty pages with J1 and some additions, and forty pages with J2 (see fig. 5.2). The last forty pages are made up of twenty from J1, sixteen from J2 (chapters 14-17) and four of redaction (18.15-27 and 21.15-25). This is the basic plan and it is carried through with remarkable precision. This chapter is concerned with the significant effects of the conflation on the final shape and content of the gospel.

1.1-2.25. In the model of the gospel this forms the first half of section one and is followed by an equal amount of material from J2.

In the general outline this was assigned to J1 but the stylometric analysis showed that the J1 source is not homogeneous and that there are large differences between and within the sequences. This suggests that this source has sometimes been transposed within the new book and intercalated with material contributed by the compiler. This is likely to be a feature particularly at the beginning of the new book. Both Matthew and Luke began their gospels with a considerable amount of heterogeneous material before drawing on their main sources to any extent and this is almost certainly true of *Acts* as well.

We have suggested that the J2 source originally existed in units of an average length of 389 letters, that it ran to 78 of these units with a possible two more embedded in 10.1-18, a total of 80 units. The unit of the J1 source appears to have been somewhat larger. The omitted *Pericope Adulterae* may be a guide. It runs to 822 letters and the calculation for a

codex in this denomination is 419.8 (see page 64). The new
book in sections two to six on this hypothesis contains 70
units of J1 and the *Pericope Adulterae* (omitted from the
gospel but included in J1) provides two more. A further three
are found in the Cleansing of the Temple (2.12-25) giving a
total so far of seventy-five units of J1, each of 420 letters. If
the document ran to eighty, then the remaining five are embedded in 1.1-2.11.

The plan of the compiler is therefore a very simple one.
He has before him two documents, one of 80×420 and one
80×389. His new codex size is 120×588 and will hold both
his sources and leave 10×588 for redaction. Thus:

$$80 \times 420 = 33,600$$
$$80 \times 389 = 31,120$$
$$\overline{}$$
$$\text{Total} = 64,720$$
$$10 \times 588 = 5,880$$
$$\overline{}$$
$$\text{Grand total} = 70,600$$

$$\text{Fourth Gospel} = 70,513$$

From the compiler's point of view the calculation is more
simple still:

$$80 \times 420 = 57 \times 588$$
$$80 \times 389 = 53 \times 588$$
$$\text{Total} = 110 \text{ units}$$

Therefore he has 10×588 of freedom.

This first section of the gospel to 2.11 accounts for eight
pages of the gospel ($8 \times 588 = 4,704$ and the observed figure
is 4,670 letters). It is significant that if the J1 source is reckoned in 420 letters, then eleven of these units run to 4,620, the
second approximate meeting point of multiples of 420 and
588. This suggests that in 1.1-2.11 there are five units of J1
and six of editorial matter.

Examining this section of text from this point of view, it is

immediately apparent that there are three natural portions
which run to twice this unit length. The first is the Prologue
(1.1-18 minus the interpolations at 6-8 and 15) of 844 letters,
the second is 1.24-34 of 837 and the third is 2.1-11 of 847.
These total to 2,528 and 6×420 to 2,520. This is unlikely to
be mere coincidence considering the precision to be found in
the remainder of the gospel.

On this assumption the new material begins with the Prologue and proceeds with the Baptist's statement regarding
one whose shoes he is unworthy to unloose (as in *Mark*
1.7-8 // *Luke* 3.16) and the descent of the spirit as a dove (as
in *Mark* 1.10 // *Matthew* 3.16 // *Luke* 3.22), followed by the
first sign at Cana. The material from J1 would then consist
of John's confession of subordination to Jesus, pointing his
disciples to Jesus as Son of God and the call of various disciples. It is easy to believe that the first interpolation at 1.6
belonged here. 1.15 is a repetition of 1.30. This method of
linking sections is not infrequent in the gospel. J1 therefore
begins 1.6-8. 14-23, 35-51.

1.19-23 (J1).   On the basis of the Isaiah quotation, used by
the Synoptics, this passage accentuates the subordinate role
of John the Baptist. He is not even 'the prophet' but only the
voice in the wilderness.

1.24-34 (R).   John foretells a superior baptism by a superior agent of God.

1.35-51 (J1).   'The next day' introduces paragraphs 1.29,
35 and 43 (followed by 'on the third day' at 2.1). Our suggestion attributes one of these to the compiler.

The emphasis on John's secondary role in 19-23 and his
direction of his disciples to Jesus (36, 37) carries the implication that John's disciples at the time of writing should follow
Jesus as did those at the beginning.

Peter is not the first to be called. He does receive the name Cephas (Rock) but there is no promise of pre-eminence comparable to that of *Matthew* 16.13-20. This position is reserved for the beloved disciple.

The Nathaniel incident has no synoptic parallel and the point seems to be that the true Israelite believes in Jesus as Son of God and King of Israel.

2.1-11 (R).   The miracle at Cana is designated the 'first of his signs'. This completes eight pages of the new book and the next incident (of two pages) prepares for the first ten pages of J2 material.

2.12-25 (J1).   The Cleansing of the Temple.
This passage raises important issues and is therefore worthy of extended comment.

Bernard[1] sums up on this incident as follows: 'Our conclusion accordingly is that there is some mistake (which cannot now be explained) in that account of the Cleansing of the Temple which places it immediately after the miracle of Cana, as the traditional text of *John* places it'. The implications of this statement are that the chronology of the gospel is or ought to be important, that in this instance it is at fault and the reason is unknown, and that perhaps the 'traditional text' is not the original.

What has happened since Bernard's time is that great efforts have been made to vindicate the chronology of the Fourth Gospel but the position which this incident occupies has remained a problem. Chronology is still considered to be important in the gospel as a whole but in this instance there is some 'mistake' from a chronological point of view. Recent commentators therefore appear to have concentrated on the second implication of Bernard's statement, namely, on finding reasons for the position of the incident in this gospel.

[1] *John* in I.C.C., vol. 1, p. xiv.

According to C. H. Dodd[2] the temple was cleansed 'almost certainly at the Passover of the Passion, the position of the pericope of the cleansing being due to the order in which the evangelist wished to present his great argument' which Dodd elsewhere describes as the 'inauguration of a new order in religion'.[3] On the same question Barrett writes: 'We may suppose either that John was in possession of an independent tradition which he rated more highly than that of Mark, or that his placing of the incident was dictated by reasons theological rather than chronological'.[4] This echoes Dodd's statement that 'for theological reasons, (he) placed the cleansing of the temple near the beginning of the series of scenes from the ministry'.[5] But if, for 'theological reasons' such an important incident can be antedated, how great is the concern for chronological order? Are there other instances in which chronology has been sacrificed to theology?

Bernard's hint that there might be a reason, not theological, has not been seriously pursued. This is to some extent due to the determination to regard the gospel as a homogeneous composition, in spite of the fact that the other major New Testament books are compiled to some degree from previously existing sources.

The most natural explanation of this kind of chronological problem in any other case would be that the writer advanced the incident from a narrative source which he was using and did so for editorial reasons. He has related the beginnings of the movement in Galilee and the miracle at Cana. He will next introduce his second source with the interviews with Nicodemus and the woman at the well. He must therefore bring Jesus to Jerusalem and the incident which effectively does this is a feast. In the source there is a journey to

---

[2] *The Historical Tradition in the Fourth Gospel*, p. 211.
[3] *The Interpretation of the Fourth Gospel*, p. 303.
[4] *John*, p. 163.
[5] *The Historical Tradition in the Fourth Gospel*, p. 162.

Jerusalem for Passover. By bringing it forward he creates the setting for the Nicodemus interview and takes in Samaria on the return journey to Galilee.

Support for this solution comes from the following considerations:

(1) 7.1-13 suggests that Jesus was not known in Jerusalem.

(2) The word 'sign' is used in the cleansing narrative but the story of the healing of the official's son at the end of chapter 4 is said to be the 'second sign', the Cana incident being the first.

(3) The introduction to the cleansing pericope is exactly similar to 11.55 which comes before the anointing: 'And the Passover of the Jews was near and he/many went up to Jerusalem'.

(4) There are other signs of disorder in the section following 11.55. In the next verse the question is asked, 'Will he come to the feast?' This is followed by the annointing, the plot against *Lazarus*, the triumphal entry. The synoptic order is the entry, the cleansing, the plot against Jesus and the annointing. It is inherently probable that the earlier extraction of the cleansing has contributed to the present order in the Fourth Gospel.

We distinguish between theological reasons for the form of the pericope and the theological reasons for its position and our concern is with the latter. If the writer saw the cleansing in the terms expounded by Dodd, there is no reason why this significance should not as fittingly attach to it at the end of the ministry. On the other hand, if editorial considerations played any part in the composition, is it not preferable to allow that they have something to do with one of the most significant chronological problems in the gospel? If modern theologians can argue that the position of the cleansing does not affect its theological significance, may not the same reasoning have influenced the writer?

2.23-25 (J1). This paragraph provides the transition to the first section of J2 by references to Jerusalem. 'At the Passover, at the feast' is awkward as is the reference to signs since none has been recorded so far in Jerusalem. The last sentence prepares for the material—'He knew what was in man. 3.1. There was a man . . .'.

3.1-4.38 (J2). Nicodemus and the Samaritan woman.
3.22-36 has the appearance of being due to the compiler at least as far as its position is concerned. Macgregor apportions it to him because it is a Baptist passage, but it cannot be assumed that J2 would never refer to the Baptist.

4.39-45 (J1). The beginning of the most anomalous section. 4.39-42 is editorial comment on the Samaritan woman incident leading to the confession of Jesus as Saviour of the World, a title which 'savours of the terminology of the mystery religions'. The next three verses form a link between the story to follow, the official's son, at Cana, and what has gone before, both in J2 (at Jerusalem) and on the occasion of the 'first of his signs', also at Cana.

4.1,2 (R). Obviously the editorial link between the Nicodemus passage and the one to follow, but very clumsily fashioned.

The order in chapters 5 to 8 (J1 and J2)

Most commentators have noted that the order in this section is very unsatisfactory. Some put this down to the writer's lack of interest in chronology. Barrett, for example, on 5.1 says regarding time and place, 'evidently John was not interested in them'. (p. 208).

The most obvious anomaly is in the relative position of chapters 5 and 6. G. H. C. Macgregor[6] states the problem as

[6] *John*, p. 124.

follows: 'The opening words of 6, "After this Jesus went off
to the opposite side of the sea of Galilee", connect admirably
with 4.54, and are perfectly natural if Jesus is at the moment
of departure (as at 4.54) near the Sea of Galilee; but they are
not appropriate after 5.47, which leaves Jesus in Jerusalem.
Further, the opening words in 7, "After this Jesus moved
about in Galilee; he would not move in Judaea, because the
Jews were trying to kill him", are not appropriate to the
position at the end of 6, where Jesus is already in Galilee, but
they would follow perfectly immediately after the account of
the visit to Jerusalem in 5'.

This situation creates greater problems for those who
regard the gospel as a homogeneous composition since there
is no textual evidence for any alternative order. But if, as we
maintain, we are dealing with a conflation, such anomalies
are readily attributable to editorial factors.

This sequence raises other problems as well. Within it
there are three references to feasts at Jerusalem, viz. 5.1;
6.4; 7.2, which are largely responsible for the discrepancy
between this gospel and the Synoptics regarding the number
of Jesus' visits to Jerusalem and the length of his public
ministry. If an editor is transposing and interpolating material, the repetition of a reference to a feast is understandable.

The mention of the Passover in 6.4 has no relevance and
is obviously editorial in intention. Barrett says that it occurs
'in order to provide an appropriate setting for the discourse
on the Bread of Life. It seems that John here introduces a
feast simply in order to account for the presence of Jesus in
Jerusalem'. (p. 209). This, of course, is the kind of argument
we have used regarding the position of the cleansing of the
temple in this gospel (see above). Whereas Barrett ascribes
the cleansing's position to theological reasons, we are consistent in attributing both to reasons arising from the needs
of the conflation.

5.1-3 is one of the most obvious editorial passages in the

gospel. It contains the common introduction to J2 material of the narrative type by reference to 'a feast of the Jews' and the condition of the text in the following verse confirms its redactional nature. The editor has adapted an incident of healing in Galilee as a setting for material which, being from J2, is sited in Jerusalem.

Most commentators find it difficult to believe that originally 7.15-24 followed 7.1-14 and some would remove 8.12-20 to follow 7.24. It is, of course, agreed that 7.53-8.11 does not belong to the text (see *pericope adulterae* below). Discontinuity is a feature of this whole section. Even if it is granted that 5.16-47 and 6.22-59 belong to a different source, the present unsatisfactory order of what remains is not affected. These two homogeneous sections are continuous individually though not consecutively and to extract them does nothing for the remainder.

Obvious discontinuities in terms of time and place are present elsewhere in the gospel in 11.54-12.26 and in chapters 14 to 16 (see below) and in the latter material also there occurs the same kind of logical discontinuity in discourse as we find in chapter 7. Its presence there suggests that since both sources show the same symptoms, this is due in both instances to the exigencies of conflation as they impinged upon the editor. The compiler felt free to transpose as well as to interpolate and he did not possess exceptional gifts in this direction. Consequently it is unlikely that attempts to discover the original order will be successful.

The material from 4.38 to 8.47, minus the two passages from the other source, runs to 20 pages. In our opinion the most likely order, if nothing has been omitted or interpolated apart from short sentences such as 6.4, may be as follows: 4.39-54; 6.1-21; 5.1-15; 7.1-14, 25-36, 15-24; 6.60-71; 7.37-52; 8.12-47. However, it is not to be expected that in the case of such transposition nothing has been altered and therefore no order will be entirely satisfactory.

7.53-8.11 (J1).   *Pericope Adulterae* omitted from gospel.

Only Codex D among early Greek manuscripts and a few old Latin manuscripts have this pericope in this position. Most of the important Greek manuscripts omit it although some leave a space after 7.52 suggesting that they knew it existed. In one manuscript it occurs after *Luke* 21.38, in another after *John* 7.36 and in some Georgian manuscripts after *John* 7.44. If it originally belonged to the Fourth Gospel, why was it omitted by some; if not, why was it included by some?

Its omission has been explained as reaction against what might seem to be a lax attitude to sexual morality in the story. This may have had some effect. On the other hand, considering the reverence in which this gospel came to be held, any interference with the text after it was generally received must have been for good reason. Such a reason could be that the story was present in one of the sources in its original form and that someone remembered this and added it to his own copy of the Fourth Gospel.

If we were to guess at its possible position in the source, it might be after 5.15 but this merely on the ground that in both of these stories the point is forgiveness pronounced by Jesus and in both the same two Greek words are used, *meketi hamartane*, 'sin no more'. If this is not the solution, it may simply be that someone who saw this relation of the two added the *pericope adulterae* into his gospel.

8.48-9.41 contains some redactional matter in verses 48-59 before the J2 story of the man born blind.

10.1-18 (J2 and R).   The Door and the Shepherd.

This passage completes the first half of the Gospel at page 60. It occurs at the end of a block of J2 to complete ten pages, the second half of a twenty-page section of which the first ten have been copied from J1. Macgregor called this a 'conglomerate' passage and added, 'As a result it is impossible to trace throughout one sequence of thought.' (p. 234).

The passage has strong affinities with the material in chapters 14-16 in three respects. Firstly, it is one of the *ego eimi* (I am) passages, secondly it is allegorical and, thirdly, as Macgregor notes, it is conglomerate. In the first two respects it is closely akin to the allegory of the vine in chapter 15 and in the third, as we have seen, it is like the rest of 14-16 in that the thought is not sequential.

These facts would lead us to suppose that this passage or part thereof comes from the same secret teaching material which the compiler uses in chapter 14 ff. and raises the question whether this was a source separate from the other non-Markan type material which starts at chapter 3. There may originally have been a separate collection of teaching purporting to have been given by Jesus to the disciples only. 10.1-18 is not connected with the material on either side of it but completes the section of twenty pages of homogeneous material. However, it is obvious that 10.19 ff. is continuous with the story of the man born blind in chapter 9. The only reason for this circumstance is editorial.

11.45-57 (R). This passage summarises the effects of the Lazarus miracle and provides the reason, according to this gospel, for the hierarchy's decision to proceed against Jesus. Dodd says that vv. 47-53 is a complete pericope and might well have reached the author as a separate unit. It is 'unlike anything else in any of the gospels'.[7] He concludes that the meeting of the council is designed 'as a pendant to the episode of Lazarus'.[8]

The thumbnail sketch of Caiaphas in which, because he occupies the office of High Priest, he is the mouthpiece of a prophecy (or oracle?) which is double edged, is likely to be later than the rest of the narrative and so probably due to the compiler as a prologue to the events of the Passover.

[7] *The Historical Tradition in the Fourth Gospel*, p. 24.
[8] *The Interpretation of the Fourth Gospel*, p. 367.

The order in 11.55-13.38

The Passion narrative begins at page 76, the start of the second half of the primary source material. 12.1b, 2b, 9-11 are editorial references to the previous incident forming a link between J2 and J1 material. The singularities of this section are well known. The two incidents of the anointing and the entry into Jerusalem, common to the Fourth Gospel and the Synoptics, are here transposed and the cleansing of the temple which the latter recount after the entry has already been included (2.11-25). The four gospels are referring to the same events but the tradition in the Fourth Gospel is considerably modified. In the anointing this gospel has given precision and detail to time, place and people involved, as in other incidents, and this generally indicates a later origin.

Here again we are faced with the decision between accepting the present order in contradiction to the synoptic tradition, or concluding that editorial re-allocation has taken place. The latter option is inevitable if we accept that the cleansing incident had already been displaced. Once again the inconsequential nature of some of the transpositions is obvious in 12.44-50 which is without context and many commentators have pointed out that Peter's question in 13.36-38 is out of place before Jesus' statement in 16.5 and is regarded as redaction.

Chapters 14 to 17 (J2)

The desire to discover secret teaching of Jesus which would give guidance in the changed circumstances of the second century led to the issue of many documents which professed to provide it. 'Jesus said' is equivalent to 'Jesus says to the church in our day'. That this is what we have in chapters 14 to 17 is obvious by many tests. The form and substance of these chapters are by no stretch of the imagination those which can be attributed to the historical Jesus.

That the order is not original is generally admitted. But even the removal of 14 to follow 16 will not give logical sequence to the section. No subject is consistently followed through. This is in contrast with 17 which is consistent and sequential. Evidently the editor did not feel competent to re-arrange what he had received as a prayer offered by Jesus.

The following distinctions are not noted as proof that 14-17 come from a separate source or that 17 is distinct from 14-16. The Fourth Gospel amounts to 15,630 words and 14-17 to 2,024, about 13%. The word *pater*, father occurs 131 times in the gospel. We might expect it to occur 17 times in 14-17 if it were uniformly distributed, but the number is 50. Similarly, the word for 'love' occurs 44 times and of these 25 are in 14-17; we should expect 3.3. (The Johannine Epistles run to 2,604 words; sixty-two are variations of the word 'love' mostly in First John, and this supports the sug-gestion that the relation between First John and the gospel refers to 14-17).

We have noted that 17 is a logical unity in contrast with 14-16. There is also an interesting contrast in their use of the words for 'send'. In 14-16 the verb is *pempo*, in 17 it is *apostello* and it occurs no fewer than seven times. All instances of *pempo* are particles, none of *apostello*.

In expositions of the leading ideas of the Fourth Gospel it is generally to this section that appeal is made. Thus Dodd on 'Eternal Life' and 'Union with God' in this gospel refers to chapter and verse sixty-five times. No fewer than sixty-one of these are to verses within 14-17.

These statistical facts regarding this section of the gospel cannot alone be used for the purpose of proving anything about the authorship of the section in relation to the rest of the gospel, but they draw attention to the impossibility of maintaining, as some commentators do, that the vocabulary is uniform throughout the gospel and that the whole is the work of one author. What these divergencies do point up is the question whether the chapters 14-17 are all from the same source and the inadvisability of maintaining that there is an affinity between First John and the whole of the Fourth Gospel.

18.15-27 (R). Peter's Denial.
The previous verse is an editorial reference back to 11.45-54. The anomalies in this passage have been obvious for a long time. Some attempts have been made to remove them by rearranging the material, the earliest probably the Sin. Syr. manuscript whose order is 12-13, 24, 14-15, 19-23, 16-18, 25. This can hardly be called successful. Macgregor, who regarded most references to Peter in this gospel as due to the redactor, attributes to him 13b to 18, 24-27.

The whole comes to two pages and it is perhaps best to regard these as compounded by the compiler who knew that he had twenty pages to fill, that his remaining material amounted to sixteen pages and that his new ending would fill two pages, thus duplicating the form of the previous twenty pages arranged as 2-16-2. The whole of 18.15-27 can be abstracted without detriment to the narrative.

18.28-21.14 (J1). Continuation and conclusion of Passion narrative.

21.15-25 (R). The New Ending
Commentators agree that 20.30, 31 is the conclusion of a book. Most see it as the conclusion of the original Fourth Gospel and chapter 21 as an addition at a later date, either by the writer or by some other hand. It is indeed the conclusion of a book but that book is the source J1 and it has been moved from an original place after 21.14 to its present position because the compiler had his own concluding sentences which would occur within two pages of the ending J1 if that were not moved.

These verses at the end of chapter 20 can be lifted from their present position without damage to the narrative. If it is supposed that their original position was after 21.14, this is very satisfactory in that 21.1-14 includes the final appearance of the risen Jesus to his disciples, designated in verse 14 'the third time that Jesus appeared to the disciples after he had risen from the dead', Mary Magdalene not being reckoned one of the disciples.

The two pages of 21.15-25 are recognised as concerned with the relative roles of Peter and the beloved disciple in the thinking of the church of the second century. The gospel gives priority to the latter as the most likely to be the repository of the true teaching of Jesus. The admission of Peter to prominence is grudging and not related to authority in doctrine. In verses 15-25 it is made clear that Peter has no part in the other disciple's appointed function. Peter is the pastor but the other, in virtue of his unique relation with Jesus, is the one who best understands the message of Jesus. Barrett sums up the intention of these pages very aptly when he says, 'Peter is the head of the evangelistic and pastoral work of the church, but the beloved disciple is the guarantor of its tradition regarding Jesus'.[9]

What the immediate implications of this may have been when the gospel was first published we can only guess. It is possible that an assertion of the priority of John implied the superiority of John's gospel over those thought to be based on the reminiscences of Peter. Beyond this, in a contest between the prominent churches for the right to be regarded as the prime centre of Christianity now that Jerusalem no longer existed as the mother church, this Fourth Gospel if widely accepted could add weight to the claim of Ephesus, provided that city is its place of origin.

The question arises, What are 'those things' referred to in verse 24 to which this disciple bears witness and on which

[9] *John*, p. 480.

he writes? If we have a book compiled from two sources plus a conclusion written by the compiler, the reference could be to either of the sources, to the conclusion, or to the complete document. If one part of the book is due to the beloved disciple as his teaching it is probably 14-17. But the impression that the whole book is the work of none other than the apostle John has been gathered from the book as it stands from the earliest times. We must therefore think it possible that this impression was intended by the compiler, perhaps to give authority to his book in view of the status already attained by the synoptic gospels.

The fact that the other gospels make no attempt to identify their writer suggests that this gospel appeared after the others and prior to the time when it became the fashion for spurious writings explicitly claiming apostolic authority to be discredited and repudiated.

Part 3

Chapter Ten

The traditional framework and the Fourth Gospel

Attempts to prove that the Fourth Gospel is indebted to any of the Synoptic Gospels have met with no success. It is certain that there is no verbal dependence of the kind which is obvious in the relation of both *Matthew* and *Luke* to *Mark*. In the opinion of Dodd, 'the presumption which lay behind much of the earlier criticism—that similarity of form and content between two documents points to the dependence of the later of these documents on the earlier—no longer holds good, since there is an alternative explanation of many such similarities, and one which corresponds to the conditions under which gospel writing began, so far as we can learn them; namely, the influence of a common tradition'.[1]

Dodd, of course, is anxious to establish the thesis that behind the Fourth Gospel lies a basic tradition which is prior to and independent of the Synoptics, hopefully even earlier and superior. This is to go to the opposite extreme and too often when the argument is evenly balanced Dodd gives his thesis the benefit of the doubt. The tradition behind the Fourth Gospel, if we are right to use this conception, is certainly different but there seems to be no way to prove (as distinct from opine) that it is earlier and better, as Dodd himself seems to realise.

What can be stated as a matter of observation is that the framework of the Fourth Gospel is that presented in the Synoptics and, by general consent, it is given initially as far

[1] *Historical Tradition in the Fourth Gospel*, C. H. Dodd, pp. 8, 9.

as our knowledge goes by the *Gospel of Mark*. There are vast differences in detail but essentially the Fourth Gospel provides the same outline to the story from the baptism of John to the empty tomb. This can be set out as follows:

		Mark	John
(1)	Ministry of the Baptist	1:2-11	1:19-36
(2)	Call of disciples	1:16-20	1:37-51
(3)	Events at Capernaum	1:21-34	4:43-54
(4)	Feeding five thousand	6:35-45	6:1-15
(5)	Walking on lake	6:45-52	6:16-24
(6)	Entry into Jerusalem	11:1-10	12:12-19
(7)	Cleansing the temple	11:15-19	2:12-22
(8)	Anointing at Bethany	14:3-9	12:1-8
(9)	Warning of betrayal	14:17-21	13:21-30
(10)	The last meal	14:22-26	13:1-30
(11)	Peter's rebuke	14:27-31	13:36-38
(12)	Gethsemane	14:32-52	18:1-11
(13)	Before the high priest	14:53-65	18:12-27
(14)	Before Pilate	15:1-15	18:28-29:16
(15)	Choice of Barabbas	15:6-11	18:38-40
(16)	Crucifixion and burial	15:21-41	19:17-42
(17)	The empty tomb	16:1-8	20:1-31

The 'omissions' from the Fourth Gospel as compared with *Mark* as a whole are considerable. *Mark* reports cures of lepers and demoniacs (of which the Fourth Gospel has none), and also provides samples of Jesus' teaching on various occasions, often in the form of parables and pithy sayings, of controversy with opponents, and one chapter devoted to apocalyptic prophecy. But nothing essential to the progress of the narrative from the banks of Jordan to the tomb in the garden is missing from the Fourth Gospel. The only divergences are at the cleansing of the temple (seven, above) and the anointing (eight, above). This gospel advances the former and reverses the order of the entry and anointing. The reason for these differences in order will be explained later.

The fact that in all other respects the traditional or Marcan framework is exactly similar, is in favour of the presumption that these displacements are the responsibility of the editor and have been made for some purpose peculiar to himself.

In detail, however, as we have already stated, the outline is treated in a vastly different fashion in the Fourth Gospel. We leave aside for the moment the considerable amount of Johannine material which cannot be assigned to the traditional framework, just as we have omitted the additional material in *Mark*. Even so the Fourth Gospel presents us with an 'enriched' version of the traditional narrative in terms both of fact and of interpretation.

Whereas *Matthew* makes use of more than 90% of *Mark* and *Luke* more than 60%, the material in the Fourth Gospel which deals with narrative referred to in *Mark* is less than 20% of *Mark*. It occurs in *John* chapters, 1, 2, 6, 12, 13, 18-20 and refers to *Mark* chapters 1, 6, 11, 14-16.8. The most obvious difference between the two is that with few exceptions the Fourth Gospel narrative is designed to convey an impression beyond the simple account of what was done or said. While *Mark* for the most part recounts an incident and leaves it to make its own impression, the Fourth Gospel is intent on making it serve as the bearer of a further meaning which is often spelled out in additional comment. If we briefly consider the outline this becomes obvious.

(1) John the Baptist is not the initiator of a national movement of repentance but a witness to Jesus, one of several. His subordination to Jesus is repeatedly emphasised.

(2) The disciples who are called first are originally followers of John as if to say, 'John was subordinate to Jesus and so should his disciples be'. Peter is brought by Andrew. The absence of John, son of Zebedee, and the later presence of the mysterious beloved disciple are complements of each other. The Fourth Gospel adds the discrete story of the call of Nathaniel.

(3) The healing of the nobleman's son in *John* is like healing stories in *Mark* but not the same as any of them.

(4) In *Mark* the feeding of five thousand is one more instance of Jesus' miraculous power. The Fourth Gospel uses it as preface to the discourse whose theme is 'I am the bread of life'.

(5) The storm on the lake is not surcharged with any meaning beyond that in *Mark* nor followed by any discourse like the previous instance. Perhaps for editorial reasons, this is the only place where one story in common with *Mark* directly follows another and where no 'use' is made of the incident.

(6) The Fourth Gospel has no account of the Marcan story of how the colt was found for the entry into Jerusalem. Both quote Psalm 118 but the Fourth Gospel goes on with a quotation from Zechariah (used also by Matthew) and a reference to future comprehension of the meaning of the event. This latter is the characteristic expression of the notion that things are not what they seem and only later will their true meaning be known, i.e. when the Fourth Gospel makes it plain.

(7) There are minor differences in the accounts of the cleansing of the temple and different reasons are given for this action. In *Mark* it is dishonest trading while in the Fourth Gospel it is the fact that the area is used at all as a 'house of business'. Neither account reveals a knowledge of what really happened which probably involved a threat to the priestly family. Once again the matter is tied up to a theological meaning in the Fourth Gospel, which again is not apparent to those present and only later to be appreciated (2:21, 22).

(8) The anointing shows differences in place, time and persons involved. It raises the question of whether a story which is worked out in detail is more reliable than one which leaves gaps in our knowledge. A coherent story may owe

something to invention whereas a ragged story may be due to the author's reluctance to go beyond what he knows. This kind of question is often raised by the characterization and dialogue of the Fourth Gospel.

(9 and 10) It is unnecessary to enumerate the differences in the account which the Fourth Gospel gives of the last meal. Here again both characterization and dialogue give verisimilitude. (The feet-washing is peculiar to the Fourth Gospel). This incident provides the setting for the four chapters of discourse which are a very distinctive feature.

(11) Incidents involving Peter are recounted in the Fourth Gospel with a certain grudging admission of his prominence. The denials at the High Priest's house are so disjointed that only editorial reasons can account for the state of the text.

(12) The Fourth Gospel reports no agony in the garden and no prayer 'that this cup might pass', nor is there any kiss from the betrayer. On the other hand it records that it was Peter who drew sword, that the *right* ear of the servant was severed and that his name was Malchus.

(13 and 14) It is noticeable that Jesus refuses to answer the High Priest but talks freely to Pilate; the opposite obtains in Mark. The effect is to emphasise Pilate's unwillingness to condemn, 'the Jews'' responsibility for the fate of Jesus and the spiritual nature of Jesus' claim to kingship.

(15) The Marcan account gives more information about Barabbas whom the Fourth Gospel describes simply as a robber. He was, according to Mark, among the rebels in prison and 'had committed murder in *the* insurrection'. There is historical interest here which is not present in the Fourth Gospel. '*The* insurrection' raises the question whether there was a revolt at the time and the fact was so well known that it could be referred to without explanation.

(16) At the cross there are a number of additions, the seamless robe, the spear-thrust, the presence of Mary, mother of Jesus, entrusting her to the beloved disciple, two

different 'words' from the cross. There is no cry of dereliction.

(17) *Mark* cuts off at 16:8. Whether it originally recounted appearances of the risen Jesus is matter for speculation. The Fourth Gospel gives a more graphic account of
the discovery of the empty tomb. In addition it records a
visit to the tomb by Peter and the beloved disciple, the
appearance to convince Thomas, the incident on the sea of
Tiberias and the commands to Peter, 'Feed my sheep' and
'follow thou me'.

It is obvious therefore that while the framework of the
Fourth Gospel is the same as that of *Mark*, there has been
no rewriting of the traditional material used by Mark as in
the case of *Matthew* and *Luke*, but a new account. Whether
this is the result of an original tradition coming to *Mark* and
the Fourth Gospel by different routes or is largely due to a
writer who put the incidents into his own perspective, is a
question yet to be answered. It would appear that the Fourth
Gospel narrative is one which has assimilated information
not available to Mark, or the writer has used considerable
powers of invention and narrative ability to give the traditional outline a new and more graphic lease of life.

There can be no doubt of the writer's ability to produce
vivid narrative, especially by characterization and dialogue.
Time and again he introduces particularity of time, place
and person as in the anointing, the description of Judas as
treasurer and thief, the identification of the right ear smitten
by Peter and the name of the victim, and various additions
at the cross and tomb. Similarly the amount of direct speech
is increased, as for example in the passages concerning the
Baptist, the call of disciples and the dialogue between Jesus
and Pilate.

Much turns on the question previously raised. Verisimilitude is not necessarily to be equated with historicity. In any
particular case the judgment can be made only on the basis

of one's estimate of whether an author in his work as a whole is or is not trustworthy in such detail. If he shows elsewhere the tendency to fill out, round off, invent circumstances or dialogue or otherwise adorn a tale, then this judgment may be adverse.

We know that in the later apocryphal gospels this is the obvious tendency. Once a factual type of accretion has attached itself to an incident in the form of particularity and dialogue it would tend to be accepted and repeated. The Fourth Gospel is certainly further along this road than the Synoptic Gospels, but whether we have here an original contribution to this tendency or acceptance of an already accreted tradition is not easy to decide. Considering that the material in the rest of the Fourth Gospel outside the framework is still further removed from bare factual narrative or from the type of teaching which fits the synoptic pattern of Jesus' words, the balance of probability is that in this document we have not a committing to manuscript of an early traditional account of the main events in Jesus' life but a new account designed to further fresh ideas of the significance of that life and the meaning of discipleship in a new age. This once again brings the Fourth Gospel to a position between the Synoptics and the later apocryphal gospels which were generally designed to propagate some doctrine dear to the heart of the writer.

Meantime two points have been made. The first is that the framework of the Fourth Gospel is the same as that of Mark which is probably based on the traditional account of the main events in the life of Jesus. The second is that nevertheless it is 'enriched' by many details which have raised questions not simply about the historical trustworthiness of this treatment of the traditional outline but about the intentions of the writer in producing this new account of the well-known events of Jesus' life.

We have confined our attention to what we believe to

have been the traditional framework of a gospel which we have been obliged to take from the oldest gospel. But the Fourth Gospel has other features which differentiate it to an even greater degree from the Synoptics. These comprise almost half of this gospel and are in the form of both events and teaching which have no parallel either in *Mark* or in the extended editions in *Matthew* and *Luke*.

Chapter Eleven

The additional Fourth Gospel material

Matthew and *Luke* have few additions to *Mark* as regards incidents, though they have considerably more didactic material in the form of parables and sayings. If we understand by incident (a) those stories which have a miraculous element and (b) encounters between Jesus and one or more persons with no miracle involved, *Matthew* and *Luke* add four of the former and six of the latter to those provided for them by *Mark*.

The four miracles are healings:

(1) The centurion's servant	*Luke* 7: 1-10, *Matthew* 8: 5-13
(2) The crippled woman	*Luke* 13: 10-17
(3) The man with dropsy	*Luke* 14: 1-10
(4) The ten lepers	*Luke* 17: 11-19

Luke has all four and *Matthew* only one while the first is the only case in which there is a remote parallel in the Fourth Gospel, i.e. the official's son (*John* 4: 43-54).

As regards the second category, confrontations between Jesus and others in which no miraculous element occurs, the six are:

(1) John the Baptist's question	*Luke* 7: 18-23, *Matthew* 11: 2-6.
(2) The Samaritan villagers	*Luke* 9: 51-56
(3) Would-be followers	*Luke* 9: 57-66. *Matthew* 8: 19-22
(4) Visit to Martha and Mary	*Luke* 10: 38-42
(5) Lament over Jerusalem	*Luke* 13: 34-35, *Matthew* 22: 57-59
(6) Zacchaeus	*Luke* 19: 1-14

Once again Luke is more successful in his additions than Matthew and in these instances there is no remote parallel in the Fourth Gospel.

In the passion narrative the only new incident is again

added by Luke, namely the confrontation between Jesus and Herod (23:6-12).

If we turn to the Fourth Gospel on the same quest, i.e. for incidents, (as distinct from didactic material) which are not to be found in *Mark* we have the following:

(1)	Call of Nathaniel	1: 43-51
(2)	Wedding at Cana	2: 1-12
(3)	Nicodemus	3: 1-21
(4)	Woman of Samaria	4: 1-42
(5)	Healing at Bethesda	5: 1-18
(6)	Man born blind	9: 1-38
(7)	Lazarus	11: 1-44
(8)	Greeks seek Jesus	12: 20-26
(9)	Feet-washing	13: 1-20
(10)	Piercing of side	19: 1-10
(11)	Peter and another at sepulchre	20: 1-10
(12)	Thomas's unbelief	20:24-29
(13)	Appearance to seven	21: 1-14
(14)	Feed my sheep	21: 15-19
(15)	Peter and the beloved disciple	21: 20-24

In addition there are extended controversies with 'the Pharisees' and 'the Jews' which have no parallel in the Synoptic Gospels and in which it is impossible to judge how much may be based on tradition and how much due to the writer.

Confining ourselves first to incident, we have already noticed that some of these are fitted to the traditional framework of a gospel. This is true of those belonging to Galilee, (1) and (2), and those which are introduced into the passion and resurrection narrative, i.e. from (9) onwards.

We are left with (3) to (8), i.e. Nicodemus (3:1-21), Samaritan Woman (4:1-42), the healing at Bethesda (5:1-18), the man born blind (9:1-38), Lazarus (11:1-44) and the quest of the Greeks (12:20-26), all having their setting outside Galilee and mainly in the Jerusalem area.

It is characteristic of these incidents not only that they are encounters between Jesus and one other, replete with dialogue, but that they are (except 8) used as pegs on which to hang a considerable amount of specific doctrine, not, as one would expect from the study of the Synoptics, about the religious customs of the day in relation to Jesus' conception of the Kingdom of God, but on the divine status of Jesus as the Son of God and the purpose for which he came into the world.

These distinctive features are sufficient to raise the question whether we have here a further distinct modification of the traditional view not only of the events but of the significance that should be attached to them and if so whether this type of material is introduced from a source which, while compatible with the Fourth Gospel treatment of the framework, is nevertheless distinct from it.

All four gospels contain narrative, miracle, teaching and controversy but the Fourth Gospel has also a large section of private discourse between Jesus and his disciples. This material is of special importance. Not only does it contribute a particular ethos to the gospel, but it raises interesting questions about the psychology of the phenomenon of *oratio recta* in relation to Jesus as the master of his disciples on the one hand and as the lord of the church on the other.

The Synoptics refer to teaching given in private but very little is recorded verbatim and that chiefly in *Matthew* 10 and *Mark* 13. The teaching of this character in the Fourth Gospel appears chiefly in chapters 14-17 and its place in the gospel is at the last meal and before the departure across the Kedron to the garden where Jesus was apprehended.

There is one large section of consecutive teaching in *Matthew* 5-7. The Fourth Gospel chapters are 14% of the whole gospel and these in *Matthew* 12%. However, it is evident that in *Matthew* we have a collection of public utterances belonging to different periods of the ministry while the Johannine matter is intended to be continuous and not merely consecutive. In addition, the subject matter in the two gospels is not similar either in style or in content. The *Matthew* section is concerned with the manner of life of those who will enter the Kingdom of God while the Fourth Gospel material deals with the nature of Jesus as revealer of the Father and the provision he makes for the future of his disciples when he himself has left the world. The style of the *Matthew* collection is entirely consistent with that attributed to Jesus in the rest of *Matthew* and the other Synoptic Gospels while the style of the Fourth Gospel teaching is, as elsewhere, impossible to disengage at sight from the general characteristics of the gospel as a whole.

As regards *Matthew* 10 and *Mark* 13, it is true that they also deal with the future of the followers of Jesus. But they refer to external events, not to the interior life of disciples. They foretell persecution, trial and even death for the sake of the gospel, enforce the duty of witnessing and propagating the message, visualise final anarchy and tribulation and an apocalyptic climax to the age. In short, they present a forecast of eschatological fulfilment of prophecy regarding the present age and the age to come. We are not concerned at the moment with how much of this can be attributed to Jesus, though it is indisputable that eschatological ideas are present elsewhere in his Synoptic teaching. The point is that the Fourth Gospel material is not capable of being embedded in the late Jewish apocalyptic ethos of pre-crucifixion Palestine in the way that the synoptic sections may be. It is written from the point of view of a different and later period. The interest is directed inward to the quasi-mystical relation between disciples and their Lord, rather than outward to the coming catastrophic denouement of history.

It is generally recognised that this material in the Fourth Gospel is not in its original order. It has suffered some form of relocation, most obviously where the last words of chapter 14—'Arise, let us go hence'—are followed by three whole chapters of speech in *oratio recta*. The most natural position for those words is before the opening words of chapter 18 which will give this sequence: '"Arise, let us go hence". Whe

Jesus had spoken these words, he went forth with his disciples over the brook Kedron'. There are other signs of disjunction which we shall note later and it is plain that whoever put 16.5 in its present position overlooked the fact that 13.36 falsifies it.

If the order is not original, the question is whether the present rearrangement was done by the original writer in revision. Now it is difficult to imagine a writer leaving his own manuscript in the present condition, though this might easily be attributed to an editor who was reshuffling another's material.

It has been suggested that the present order may be due to a mechanical accident such as misplacement of a page. This suggestion presupposes a codex form. This in itself is no objection. The earliest manuscript of the New Testament is the Rylands fragment 3.45.7 and it comes from a codex of *John*. But such an accident would require that the particular page or pages contained nothing more or less than a section that would fit and would neither begin nor end in the middle of a sentence. If one deliberately sets out to find such a page in any written manuscript or indeed in any printed volume, one experiences great difficulty. That it should happen by chance is most unlikely. A close parallel to the present situation may be the relation between chapters 5 and 6. The likelihood is therefore that the rearrangement is by another hand and not by accident and that it was carelessly done as far as detail is concerned.

This being so, the further question then emerges: Were parts of this private discourse of Jesus not merely displaced within the section but detached and inserted elsewhere in the gospel? This is not unlikely when we consider the lack of historical continuity in other places and the fact that the primary interest is didactic. Such a passage as the allegory of the door and the shepherd in chapter 10 has the same qualities as the allegory of the true vine in chapter 15.

C. H. Dodd says of the chapters we are considering that they are 'among the most characteristic, the most original, and the most highly wrought of all the passages in which this evangelist has presented the religious and theological core of his message'.[1] We may not be in a position readily to say what is 'characteristic' of the Fourth Gospel if it is a composite work, but the reason for introducing this reference is the fact that Dodd recognises that it is the work of the 'evangelist' and presents the core of 'his' message. If this were freely recognised it would soon be apparent that attempts to found it on *ipsissima verba* of Jesus are foredoomed to failure, just as the spurious attempt to prove that the Fourth Gospel contains parables. This latter is carried out by extending the word parable to include any short metaphorical saying and then showing that there are some of these in the Fourth Gospel.[2] But no stories such as those in the Synoptics that we call parables can be found in the Fourth Gospel.

Accepting that this material which appears as the private discourse of Jesus is in fact the composition of someone living in a quite different milieu a long time after, the more interesting question is—how does a writer come to find himself in the position where he can write, 'Jesus said', and proceed to put his own words on the lips of Jesus?

Suppose we dismiss at once the deliberate intention to deceive. Even the writer of the *Acts* of Paul may be credited with nothing more culpable than guileless enthusiasm when he confessed that he had written it only out of love for Paul. There were instances of deliberate deception, perpetrated for reasons that were more or less discreditable, and the church of the late second century was not slow to make accusations to this effect. This applied to the whole range of Christian literature of the period—Gospels, Epistles, Apocalypses— and even to some administrators and historians. Burckhard

---

[1]   C. H. Dodd, *Historical Tradition in the Fourth Gospel*, p. 52.
[2]   A. M. Hunter, *According to John*, chapter 8.

must have had some provocation to call Eusebius of Caesarea 'the foremost conscious liar in history'.

But there is no need to impute base and deceitful motives in every case when we come across this literary phenomenon in which the reported speech of a character cannot be regarded as his *ipsissima verba*. The motives and purposes may be quite unexceptional and indeed the operation may serve great ends. In the limited area of exact historical science only is it necessary to be clear about the distinction between what was actually said and intended and the second-hand report of an author using his own words in the conviction (which may, of course, be mistaken) that he is conveying the sense and significance of the occasion. Classical writers who themselves wrote the speeches which they attributed to prominent characters were not deceiving themselves at least, and their reading public probably recognised this as a liberty that ought to be conceded to such authors. The age did not make an imperious demand for the truth, the whole truth and nothing but the truth.

It may be argued, however, that such a fine distinction between actual and attributed speech was made in the case of the words of Jesus and that this was one of the factors in the exclusion of many works from the canon. The words of Jesus ought to be as reliable to the Christian as the five books of Moses to the Jew. This is true or rather it came to be true. The important question is, how soon did it come to be true? The Fourth Gospel is perhaps significant in this respect as in many others that it may have been written and published at the time when this criterion was only in process of formation. The fact that it was only with some initial difficulty that it was included in the canon of gospels may support this view. Certainly it is the case that no other later gospel, however high the authority it claimed, was canonised.

The psychological history of the phenomenon with which we are concerned probably goes back a long way in both the

Hebrew and the Greek tradition. In Old Testament and inter-
testamental prophecy the man of God frequently speaks in
the name of God in *oratio recta*. The Greeks also believed
that the gods spoke through certain inspired men such as
poets and rhapsodists in direct utterance. The subject is dis-
cussed in Plato's *Ion*. We may believe that it began with men
who genuinely experienced prophetic trance and spoke under
the influence of what was considered divine afflatus. The
distinction between this and profound conviction is not easy
to judge.

In the early church there was a definite place for the prophet and it can well be imagined that some were moved to
use the direct form of speech in telling their audience what
Jesus was saying to the church in their day. All the circumstances of the time known to us permit it and in particular
the belief that the living Lord speaks to his people through
the spirit. Paul himself claimed that his knowledge was not
confined to what he had heard about the teaching of Jesus
but was based on a revelation from the glorified Christ who
spoke to him and whose word he conveyed to the churches.[3]
This conception is basic to the book of *Revelation*, for example, and in A.D. 170 Melito, Bishop of Sardis, uses the
same method. Speaking in the name of the risen Lord he
prefaces his words with 'He arose from the dead and then
cries to you, saying,' etc.

There is an interesting passage in Origen[4] where he says,
'I have read somewhere (he probably refers to the apocryphal *Gospel of Thomas*) that the Saviour said—and I wonder
whether someone has fictitiously assumed the role of the
Saviour, or has recalled these words from memory, or if it is
true that this was said—that the Saviour said, He who is
near me is near the fire; he who is far from me is far from the
kingdom'. Here Origen is aware of the dilemma created by
the phenomenon we are considering.

[3] Cf *Galatians* 1:11-19; *1 Corinthians* 7:10,12,25; 11:23 ff.
[4] Origen, *Jer. Hom.* 20.3.

Regarding the gnostics of the second century, R. M. Grant writes: 'Since they believed that they possessed the true understanding of Jesus' teaching, they felt free to restate what he had taught so that its gnostic significance would become clear'.[5] But this tendency was not the exclusive preserve of gnostics. Anyone who believed he really understood the meaning of the teaching of Jesus was liable to the same temptation. The writer of the passages we are considering was possessed of such a conviction in a high degree. It is plain from many parts that there is a strong underlying notion that the teaching of Jesus was not fully understood till the writer's time, if not actually only by the writer himself.

There is also this further factor, namely, the belief that the full revelation brought by Jesus was not given in his public teaching but in private conversation with the inner circle of his disciples. This notion is present in the synoptic tradition, e.g. in *Mark* 4.11 where Jesus tells the disciples that the secret of the kingdom belonged to them but 'for those who are without, all things are done in parables'. There was therefore a belief that the intimate apostles alone could impart the full truth of the teaching. Compare Papias' statement that he was eager to hear from the lips of those who had had personal contact, what any of the apostles had said.

It was not surprising therefore that there grew up a belief that only those who received a revelation which had been given to a few select disciples and handed down secretly would be saved. This to some degree explains the popularity of apocryphal gospels which claimed to provide such material. Among the Nag Hammadi books are apocalypses of John, James, Paul and Peter, all represented as transmitting secret teaching. There are also the *Gospel of Truth*, the *Gospel of Philip* and the *Gospel of Thomas*. The last mentioned begins: 'These are the secret words which Jesus the

[5] R. M. Grant, *The Secret Sayings of Jesus*, p. 89.

living Lord spoke and Didymus Judas Thomas wrote'. In such circumstances a gospel purporting to come from one whom Jesus loved and who reclined next to him at supper in the most favoured position would certainly be irresistible.

Undoubtedly a most powerful inducement to put words into the mouth of Jesus was the fact that no higher authority existed in the church than the command or instruction of the Lord. With the passage of time the authentic words no longer met the new situation. This was most notably true when the expectation of the parousia was dying out. The church believed that the risen Lord gave the Holy Spirit to guide it from age to age and therefore authentic guidance (on which the first epistle of John has something to say) was equivalent to the word of Jesus for the time. It was 'what the spirit was saying to the churches'. The word of apostles has some weight in proportion as it was believed to be based on the word of Jesus but the word of Jesus was paramount. Paul makes the distinction between his own advice and the word of the Lord. Later the written word of an apostle was accorded the same kind of authority as the word of Jesus since it was through the apostles that the genuine word of Jesus was transmitted. Hence the authority of the apostles is the reason for apocryphal apostolic letters as the word of Jesus is the reason for apocryphal gospels.

The temptation to stretch the concept to include the writer's notion of what the apostle or the Lord would say in the given circumstances was all but irresistible and there is the question of how far the writer should go to persuade the reader that the word of instruction he is being given really has the authority of the apostle or the Lord. In the deutero-Pauline letters the authority of Paul is claimed for the doctrine they contain and there are no inhibitions about attributing them to the apostle. How far this was recognised as a convention is difficult to say. In the inter-testamental period literature of a pseudonymous nature was so extensive that

few readers could have been so naïve as to accept the osten-
sible authorship. But this kind of discrimination did not arise
in the church till the second century by which time the
'received' books had an assured position.

It would appear that the practice in the first instance was
to attribute the words purporting to come from Jesus to the
risen Lord, speaking to his church by his spirit, as in the case
of the Apocalypse and in the introduction to the *Gospel of
Thomas* quoted above. The step from that to crediting the
advice or doctrines, considered appropriate to a period fifty
or one hundred years after his death, to Jesus in his lifetime,
is not inconsiderable and could not have been taken in a fit
of absentmindedness. Once taken, however, it was sure to
become a popular form of propagating new ideas both in
doctrine and in practice. This is the intention of most if not
all of the pseudonymous writings. It is true that the Synoptic
Gospels may not be altogether blameless in this respect. It is
difficult to estimate how far the actual words of Jesus have
been modified or new ones invented to be relevant to a post-
crucifixion situation particularly in *Matthew* and *Luke*. But
this is not a prime motive as it is in later writings. Once
again, the Fourth Gospel lies somewhere between the two
extremes.

If we summarise the motives leading to the literary phenomenon of attributing to Jesus teaching which could belong
only to a later period they are principally three—the belief
that the full revelation was given by Jesus to the apostles in
private instruction, the belief that the Spirit is the *alter ego* of
Jesus and the word of the Spirit is the word of Jesus, the
belief that the way to give authority to new thinking about
the doctrine and practice of the Church is to convince
readers that the new teachings are the word of Jesus the
living Lord, or, more ambitiously, the word secretly spoken
to his disciples in the days of his flesh. These motives are
very evident in the thinking behind the Fourth Gospel and in

particular the section we are now considering. Jesus here reveals things that are not understood there and then but will be seen to be full revelation in a future time when the Spirit brings them to the Church's remembrance, which time is that moment when the gospel is being written and sent into the world. In this section more than anywhere else in the gospels, the Holy Spirit is the equivalent of the presence of Jesus with his church and his function is to recall and to reveal. Here, as we have seen, we have a large section of a gospel devoted to private instruction which is obviously considered to be of paramount importance to the church of the day. Since this material cannot be regarded as the *ipsissima verba* of Jesus, it must be regarded as conveyed in this form with a view to giving it the authority which the *ipsissima verba* of Jesus would naturally have. This is, if not the first instance of the deliberate use of this method, at least the earliest in Christian literature known to us.

The overall theme of these secret discourses is what Jesus means to his church at the time of writing when he is no longer present in bodily form. In other words, given that the crucifixion, resurrection and ascension are long past and that the hope of a parousia such as was expected in the earliest days of the church has faded, or at the least is not an immediate prospect, what does it now mean to be a follower of Jesus? Broadly speaking the answer is union with Jesus (through faith, knowledge and obedience) who is the revelation of the Father and himself the Son in union with the Father.

The prayer which comprises chapter 17 has on the face of it all the appearance of being composed at a sitting. The writer has with great success performed the difficult feat previously referred to of projecting or rather retrojecting himself into the pre-crucifixion situation from which he then looks forward in history to his own day. Perhaps there is some slight advance on the road between history and prophecy in going beyond the 'Jesus says' to 'Jesus lifted up his eyes to heaven and said, the hour is come', etc., but it is probably not noticeable if both equally are followed by words which belong to the author. Only in two other places outside chapter 17 is the direct, 'Father' (vocative) used by Jesus—in 11.41, where it is also preceded by the lifting up of the eyes, and in 12.27, 28 (twice). This alone, of course, can tell us little regarding the relation between these chapters as regards authorship.

The prayer is an orderly progression—for himself (1-5), for his immediate disciples (6-19) and for the future disciples 'who believe in me by their word' (20-26). The rest of this material is not characterised by the same logical consistency. There are at least seven sub-topics which leapfrog over one another throughout the section 14-16 and four of them are also related to chapter 17. It looks as if only clumsy editing could account for the order or rather lack of order in the present arrangement of the material.

The seven sub-topics are:

(1) Jesus' departure, its effect on the disciples, the reasons for it, the benefits that follow.
  14.1-4, 18, 19, 26-28;   16.5-7, 16-22;   17.13.
(2) The intimate relation between the Father and the Son.
  14.5-14, 20;   16.28;   17.1-8.
(3) Love, belief and obedience to Jesus' command.
  14.15, 21, 23-24;   15.9-15, 17;   17.23.
(4) The Paraclete-Spirit, his nature and functions.
  14.16, 17, 26;   15.9-15, 17;   17.23.
(5) Jesus in and for his disciples.
  14.20;   15.1-17;   17.9-19, 26.
(6) Persecution by the world, succour by Jesus.
  15.18-25;   16.1-4, 33.
(7) Asking in Jesus' name.
  14.13-14;   16.23-27.

The state of this text strongly suggests drastic editorial interference and that by someone whose mind is very different from the mind of the writer of chapter 17. It is difficult to imagine an original writer composing in snippets, his mind shooting back and forth over a limited number of subjects so that no one theme is followed out consistently. At the same time what editor would, for instance, split up the teaching on the Paraclete in the way that is done here? What we may have is original material trimmed and added to by an inferior editor. If we take the text as it stands we are left with the choice between an inconsequential author or an editor who was capable of relating words but not ideas. Since the text is not in order as a whole (14.31 and 16.5 certainly being out of position where they are), and since chapter 17 is consistent and the product of an orderly mind, the second alternative is preferable but the truth may be even more complicated.

The breaking up of a consistent discourse by the introduction at intervals of material which is cognate but not directly relevant might be the reason for the impression of diffusion in 8.20-59 and 10.1-18. In the former the consistent subject is the contrast between Christ, the Son of God the Father, and the Jews, who are of their father the devil; in the latter the consistent subject is Christ, the good shepherd. The introduction in the former case of the idea of Abraham as the father of the Jews and in the latter of Christ as the door of the sheepfold, while not incongruous are nevertheless distractive and raise the same question as to whether the original form has been subject to editorial interference.

Generally speaking, the theologian will prefer to find some profound meaning in the text which he is expounding, provided he can detect no obvious change in style within it. But there is no way in which he can distinguish between a homogeneous passage, the work of one mind, and the passage which is the result of compilation with the intention that it should be received as homogeneous. He should therefore be prepared to consider the possibility that some passages belong to the latter category if a hiatus in the thought is present, especially if he is committed to the conclusion that the document concerned is not by the author by whom it purports to be written or does not have the homologation it it professes to have.

Perhaps an analogy with the corpus of Isaiah is not inapt. The scholars of the nineteenth century discovered that what had hitherto been accepted as the work of one prophet was in fact a corpus of writings from a number of different hands set down over a considerable period of time. The signs of unity were due not to unity of authorship but to the continuous work of a school of disciples, of whom the most notable was the writer of the bulk of *Isaiah* 40-48.

Confusion is present in the traditions regarding the authorship of the Fourth Gospel; not only are there references to John, son of Zebedee, John the Elder and 'John' the beloved disciple but an early fragment[6] recounts that 'John' urged 'his fellow-disciples and his bishops' to pool their information and that it was revealed to Andrew that 'John should write down all things under his own name'. We recall also that there is a corpus of Johannine literature on which scholars are not agreed regarding authorship (e.g. both Dodd and Barrett dispute the identity of authorship of First John and the gospel). In the light of these facts it does not seem an improbable suggestion that all four documents emanate from a close circle or school and that their present shape is due to the devoted labours of fellow-disciples. One of them made the most characteristic contribution but the gospel as we have it is not as it first took form. At the turn of the century Loisy[7] gave this opinion on the literary structure of

---

[6] *The Muratorian Canon*, dated c. 180 A.D.
[7] Alfred Loisy, *The Origins of the New Testament*, p. 205.

the Fourth Gospel: 'The fact is that while the Fourth Gospel, at one stage of its compilation, was constructed on an orderly plan, there has been considerable dislocation of the plan in subsequent redaction'.

Chapter Twelve

Theologian's dilemma

Hebrew religion is distinctive in the emphasis it places on God's revelation of himself in history. It is true that the whole of creation spoke to the Hebrew of the creator but the formative influence in Hebrew theology is what God is believed to have done for his people in their historical development through the centuries, particularly in such specific events as the exodus, the giving of the law, establishing the kingdom, the exile, the return. He was known by what he had done, by his mighty acts.

This is the context in which it is possible to understand Judaism's extraordinary reverence for scripture, the written record of Israel's past, and its extreme deference to tradition, which is simply the insistence that God will never be unfaithful to his own nature as revealed in his past dealing with his people.

The literary account of these events, Israel's account of her own history in her scriptures, in due course became equivalent to an authoritative revelation of God and of his will for his people, the basis of a closed system of religious truth. It was not the unadulterated and unillumined record of the past but a stereotype of the actual course of history, just as the traditional patriotic history of Rome was, for example, in the time of Livy. Israel saw her history in a particular way, that is, through the lens of her belief that God was acting for her and in her through historical happenings.

As the offspring of Judaism, Christianity inherited this ability to find the revelation of God in historical event. It took over the idea that God is a God who acts and crowned it in the belief that his cardinal action took place in the life of

157

Jesus who was not only the Jewish Messiah but the agent of God's action on behalf of all men.

The literary record of this cardinal event, the church's gospels, came to occupy a parallel place in Christianity to that of the Old Testament in Judaism. That is to say that the gospels provided, in time, the stereotype of the story of Jesus on which its system of religious truth depended.

Now the historical question, the question of what actually happened in the history of Israel or the story of Jesus, is raised from outside the Hebrew or Christian tradition. The believer does not question the stereotype. For him it is the history, it is what actually happened and it is the bearer of the revelation of God. But the historical question, though it is not asked by the man who seeks religious conviction, is nonetheless legitimate. However disturbing it may be to faith, it is not possible to forbid the question: 'Did such an event take place as and when the faithful believe it to have taken place?' and indeed the further question: 'How, if in any way, is the religious conviction, related to the event, affected by the answer?'.

In this area the Fourth Gospel is a unique subject since it raises the question of the relation between the stereotype and history in its most acute form and at an early stage of Christian history. There is evidence that when this gospel was first published, before it became an important component of the stereotype, it was not universally welcomed. Indeed it was vigorously repudiated in certain quarters. Not till Theodore of Antioch (c. 180) was it definitely quoted as scripture written by the apostle John. There is no doubt that the supposed authorship was a powerful influence in making it acceptable.

Further, it was quite early recognised that this gospel raised the question of historical accuracy in a disturbing fashion when it was placed alongside the Synoptics. Although incongruities were ultimately treated either as enrichments of the tradition or as matters of minor importance, they were noted and remarked on.

Origen,[1] for instance, regarded variety in the accounts of Jesus' life as means of extending the range of the spiritual meaning of the gospels. The spiritual implications of the story might even sometimes be more effectively presented by disregarding mere chronological sequences. Theodore of Mopsuestia[2] adopted another attitude when he recognised grades of authority and regarded *Matthew* and *John* as more authoritative than *Mark* and *Luke* on the ground that the former were the work of disciples. (This argument is used by Eusebius[3] also). The Synoptics, in Theodore's view, have no real chronology; it is John who gives precise dates and times. In the passion narrative, only he could give an eye-witness account at certain points.

It is important to recognise that both Origen and Theodore conceived their task as reconciling the Fourth Gospel with the Synoptics and justifying its position as a component of the stereotype. What they could not do was to accept, or assume for the sake of argument, the proposition that the Fourth Gospel was purely and simply historically untrustworthy. This is to say that the real historical question was merely uncovered but its significance was not realised. Nor could it be till the rise of genuine historical criticism. However difficult it was to make one story out of the four, this is what had to be done since there could be only one stereotype and the stereotype was believed to be the history. Within the household of faith the radical difficulties could not be appreciated.

With the rise of historical criticism in the modern period, the Fourth Gospel became a subject of controversy and that very understandably. A massive defence of the traditional

---

[1] *Origen*, ed. A. E. Brooks, Frag. 74; 6.39; 19.19.
[2] Theodore of Mopsuestia, Series 4, Vol. 3, 244, 34-245, 7.
[3] Eusebius, Book 111, Chapter 24.

view of the gospel as an integral part of the historically trust-worthy record of the life and teaching of Jesus, written by an intimate disciple, was psychologically inevitable. The truth of the faith was believed to depend on the historical revel-ation in the life of Jesus which was authentically known through the written record. Any questioning of the reliability of the record could only be seen as inimical to the faith.

In this country this defence found classical expression in the commentary by B. F. Westcott[4] with its 'concentric proof' that the gospel was written by a Palestinian, a Jew, a disciple of Jesus, none other than the apostle John. It was therefore trustworthy. This defence was concerned primarily with the needs of believers. It was, however, assumed that it also answered the historical question. This assumption was made because the message of Christianity was taken to include belief that the stereotype story of Jesus was not other than the history of Jesus.

In fact, the historical question, 'Is the Fourth Gospel an account of the life and teaching of Jesus as lived out in Palestine?' could not be answered affirmatively. However successful theologians might be in proving that the theology of the Fourth Gospel is an inevitable and necessary inter-pretation of the meaning of Jesus, this was not equivalent to saying that the Jesus of the Fourth Gospel is the Jesus of the Synoptics and both together are a transcript from history.

The further investigation proceeded the more obvious this became. But worse was to follow. The historical investigation led not only to questioning the historicity of the Fourth Gospel but to asking whether the Synoptics provided the basic material for a trustworthy historical account of the life of Jesus. In short, it began to be fully realised that the stereo-type of faith is a stereotype, that there is no certainty about the congruity of the story as traditionally received and the actual 'way in which things really happened', that, in Bult-

[4] B. F. Westcott, *The Gospel according to St. John.*

mann's terms, faith cannot be at the mercy of history or dependent on the historian's ability to provide certainty about historical events as its own necessary foundation.

To most scholars, however, this appeared to be too radical a departure from tradition. Paradoxical as it may seem, it has been possible for some New Testament scholars to find comfort even in the fact that all four gospels were on the same footing, none primarily historical though related to history, all four primarily proclamation of the Christian view of the life and teaching of Jesus. Their reasoning was not that history provides no apologetic for faith but that the historical argument can now be maintained over the whole of the gospel area but in an attenuated form.

The argument takes this kind of shape. If the gospels are not history, they are inexplicable apart from history. If they are not directly evidence of God at work in the sense of a typescript of what actually happened, they are testimony to the fact that God has been at work. Consequently where questions about the historical foundations of the faith are legitimate, the Fourth Gospel may equally well with the Synoptics have something to contribute as to the presuppositions on which they are all based.

This is a tenable position if those who hold it realise how far they have moved from the traditional view that the stereotype is the history. Unfortunately it is a position which has tended to be misrepresented so that it appears to be a re-affirmation of the thesis that fundamentally and with negligible qualifications the stereotype may still be taken as if it were the history. If it can be proved that in some respects the Fourth Gospel is historically credible, it is argued, this can be extended to mean that its basis in history is sufficient to rebut the possible objection that for the life of Jesus it is historically unreliable.

There followed a minute examination of the Fourth Gospel with this in view and some prophecies of the re-

instatement of the gospel as not only theologically but historically dependable 'to some extent', a rider which tended to be
ignored. It was often assumed that, if a case could be made
out that a number of minor details were possibly authentic,
this was equivalent to providing the whole gospel with the
authentic marks of historical reliability, as, for example, that
if the writer knew something of the topography of Palestine
his story was therefore entitled to be regarded as trustworthy
—a manifest *non sequitur*.

In 1956 T. W. Manson[5] claimed that 'there is a growing
body of evidence that the Fourth Gospel enshrines a tradition of the ministry which is independent of the synoptic
accounts, bears distinct marks of its Palestinian origin and
is on some points quite possibly superior to the synoptic
record'. We should note that the concern here is with the
fundamentally historical question, Is the stereotype the
history? and that the surmise, for it is no more, is that the
Fourth Gospel may provide 'independent', 'Palestinian' and
'quite possibly superior' information. Theodore and Westcott are within hailing distance. But even if it were proved
beyond question that there is independent and Palestinian
material in the gospel, how is it then proved to be superior?

J. B. Higgins[6] wrote, 'It is possible, not so much perhaps
that the gospel itself is a finished product, but that its
sources or traditions are no later and even earlier than the
synoptic tradition'. Here is a fine combination of discretion
and rashness, adding up to the confident guess. The implication is that if the case were proved it would amount to
something of consequence. But what?

The form of such statements indicates that there is more
hope than proof. Neither of these writers believes that he has
been able to separate and identify the sources of the Fourth

[5] T. W. Manson, *The Background of the New Testament and its
Eschatology*, p. 219.
[6] J. B. Higgins, *The Historicity of the Fourth Gospel*.

Gospel and establish which are more or less trustworthy historically. Both have indicated a longed-for advance towards a belief in the basic historicity of the book 'on some points' and 'in its sources and traditions', but in the scholarly way that leaves the door open for a swift retreat. They are anxious to avoid the possibility which Bultmann, for instance, is ready to meet, namely, that the traditional assumptions about the historical life and teaching of Jesus are not only not verifiable but may in some respects be quite mistaken.

If we review the history of Fourth Gospel criticism, the traditional concern of theologians has been expressed as an impulse to maintain the trustworthiness of the Fourth Gospel as being true as history, which failing, true to history. The idea that the story of Jesus is legendary and that nothing corresponding to it actually happened would be fatal to the traditional faith. The notion that the gospel message is purely speculative and quite unrelated to the life and teaching of a real person would radically affect some presuppositions of the Christian religion. The relation between what is believed to have actually happened and the message, if not one of identity, must at least be one of interdependence.

If it could be said that the Fourth Gospel is a transcript from history and its message simply a recital of the salient events, this would obviously be an impregnable position from this point of view. This never has been the situation, nor indeed could be, however long and devoutly it was held to be. To the time of Westcott it was still thought essential to argue that the Fourth Gospel was the work of an eye-witness, none other than the apostle John and that both narrative and teaching could be relied on.

Once this line of apologetic is abandoned, it becomes all the more necessary from the traditional point of view to prove that the gospel is at least true to history. If it cannot be taken as a work from which to learn 'the course of events', it must at least be true to the course of events, or, as it is sometimes expressed, 'based on authentic historical material'.

This second line of argument arises while it is still possible to regard the Synoptics as providing the essential historical foundation to the message and therefore while it is still possible to believe that the necessary historical 'facts' of the life of Jesus are available. It therefore takes the form of trying to prove that at the base of the Fourth Gospel lies the same kind of traditional material as is found in the Synoptics and, in particular, in the earliest stratum to be discovered. However developed, interpreted, extrapolated, it is the same material that is being used.

At first it seemed that the most obvious way of securing this position was by proving that the writer of Fourth Gospel depended to some degree on *Mark* or had before him and subsumed into his Gospel the essential elements of *Mark*. Charnwood[7], for example, believed that the Fourth Gospel 'is written, so to speak on the top of St. Mark'. Streeter[8] had no doubt of this but adds that 'the materials he uses have all been fused in the crucible of his creative imagination, and it is from the image in his mind's eye, far more vivid than the written page, that he paints his picture'. This latter view poses the question how far historical material which has been worked over by another writer's 'creative imagination' could remain historical.

Of recent years, however, this kind of problem has been by-passed since confidence in the preposition that the Fourth Gospel used *Mark* has been eroded. R. H. Fuller[9] writes: 'Previously even the slightest verbal resemblances were thought to be sufficient to warrant the conclusion of direct literary dependence. The trend today is to require a high

---

[7] Lord Charnwood, *According to St. John*.
[8] B. H. Streeter, *The Four Gospels*.
[9] R. H. Fuller, *The New Testament in Current Study*, pp. 123, 4.

percentage of verbal agreement plus agreement in order before concluding literary dependence'. Both Dodd and Bultmann deny any literary dependence of the Fourth Gospel on *Mark*.

The new line of argument took the unlikely form that certain items of Fourth Gospel material which have no parallel in the Synoptics, nevertheless come from the same early stratum of tradition. The material needed to prove such a case is necessarily lacking. It is conjecture and no more and whether it is acceptable will depend largely on how eagerly one wishes it to be true.

C. H. Dodd[10] concludes an argument of this kind as follows: 'Such examples allow of no positive inference, but they may rightly serve as a warning against a hasty assumption that nothing in the Fourth Gospel has any claim to be regarded as part of the early tradition of the sayings of Jesus'. Anyone who would wish to use this as part of an argument for the historicity of the Fourth Gospel even in this small section of its composition is in very desperate straits.

There is one more type of argument which tries to secure a link between the Fourth Gospel and the earliest traditions about Jesus. All attempts at establishing continuity with written and oral material of a probably trustworthy character having proved inconclusive, the resort is to conjecture, based on historical understanding of Jesus' life. This is, however, subjective in the extreme. It depends on personal estimates of what may have been possible in the circumstances and also on what may have been possible in the life of one who was to some extent unique and whose actions therefore may be relatively unpredictable.

Goguel[11], for instance, has attempted this kind of conjecture with a view to establishing the historicity of the Fourth Gospel at some points where it diverges from the

[10] C. H. Dodd, *Historical Tradition in the Fourth Gospel*, p. 431.
[11] M. Goguel, *Life of Jesus*, Chapter 4.

Synoptic tradition. He makes a judgment that in certain instances the Fourth Gospel is more likely to be right than the Synoptic tradition. He thinks it probable that two of Jesus' disciples were originally followers of John the Baptist (1.35-42), that there was a Judaean ministry prior to the Galilaean (3.22), that a Messianic demonstration followed the feeding of the multitude (6.15), that Jesus was in Jerusalem and its environs during the last six months of his life (7.14-11.54), that the last supper took place on 13 Nisan and that Jesus did appear before Annas, the real though not the nominal wielder of high priestly power (18.13).

These are propositions which would be differently assessed by different scholars. Some would be considered likely, such as that one or two of Jesus' disciples previously followed John as indeed did Jesus himself since, according to the Synoptics, he accepted John's baptism. A Messianic outburst is problematical and depends on what the likelihood is that Jesus was recognised as Messiah in his lifetime and if so what was the form and content of such a belief.

Recently there has been considerable support for the Fourth Gospel date of the last supper but Barrett[12], for example, is not convinced and of the appearance before Annas this writer says, rather ambiguously, 'no reliance can be placed on his (the Fourth Gospel) version of the story (though probably numerous historical details remain in it)'.

From the point of view of assigning reliable historical data to those parts of the Fourth Gospel which are not covered by the Synoptic Gospels the upshot is entirely unsatisfactory. The total additional advance on the knowledge of the historical Jesus to be derived from the Synoptics could not be anything but negligible.

The primary materials for the activity of Jesus, therefore, remain the Synoptic tradition, however that may have been altered by the theological intention by which it is informed.

[12] C. K. Barrett, *The Gospel According to John*, p. 438.

Where this material is contradicted in the Fourth Gospel there are few instances indeed in which scholarship assigns the balance of probability to this gospel. Where new material is being offered by the Fourth Gospel, there is no certainty that it is traceable to a reliable primitive tradition or, if so, that it contributes materially to the already existing picture derived from the Synoptics. In short, the effect is to confirm the view that the Fourth Gospel is at least one remove further from the facts and circumstances of Jesus' life than are the Synoptics.

The consequences for a theology which assumes that the Fourth Gospel is intended to be true as history, or even true to history in the same degree as the Synoptics, should be obvious. It is not possible to maintain the Hebrew logic of historical fact encapsulating revelation, transferred to written record, issuing in certainty to the believer in historical terms. Indeed we are forced to doubt, even in the case of the Hebrews, (although this is the logic of their apologetic and of their attitude to scripture and tradition), that faith in God and knowledge of his will is explainable as a deduction from historical event. The stereotype given in scripture is never simply the record of what happened in history. From this point of view the whole attempt to excogitate historical trust-worthiness may be seen to be a blunder initiated by the misguided desire to prove that the assurance which is faith has its basis in historical necessity. It is almost certain that the writer and compiler of the Fourth Gospel did not have this as a master premiss.

The evidence is that this gospel was put together by a different process from that exemplified in *Mark* and with a different intention. *Mark* is of traditional growth and didactic in purpose; the Fourth Gospel is created to propagate a particular theological habit of mind rather than to convey factual information. They are related in the kind of way that the stories of Arthur relate to Tennyson's *Morte d'Arthur*.

Both in the manner of its formation and in its pragmatic function *Mark* is indigenous to Palestinian Judaism. The Fourth Gospel is Hellenistic in ethos and in intellectual motive, in spite of its Palestinian subject matter. It is the marriage of this ethos and intention with a gospel of Jewish origin which makes this book unique. Any Hellenistic reader familiar, for example, with the Greek author's method of composing speeches appropriate to the intention of his book, would never make the mistake of supposing that Jesus' speeches in the Fourth Gospel were or were intended to be verbatim reports. Only the assimilation of the document into a canon of Jewish provenance could make such a proposition seem possible.

In 1906 F. C. Burkitt[13] wrote of this gospel: 'The evangelist was no historian. Ideas, not events, were to him the true realities and if we go to his work to learn the course of events we shall only be disappointed'. It is true that at this time Burkitt could feel secure in the thought that 'the course of events' was adequately represented in the Synoptic Gospels. Since to some extent this assurance has ebbed away, some scholars have felt it all the more necessary to avoid the full force of Burkitt's verdict but have succeeded only in confirming it.

The deficiencies of the Fourth Gospel as a historical document are not simply those which have to do with matters of miracle like turning water into wine and the raising of Lazarus. Historical untrustworthiness is not a judgment which springs from an inability to believe in the miraculous and can therefore be dismissed as the product of nineteenth-century scientism. It is such facts as the artificiality of the setting, the lack of genuine knowledge about or interest in how life was lived in first-century Palestine, its cultural, economic and religious setting, that betray the lack of historical purpose. The intention to be historical is not there.

[13] F. C. Burkitt, *The Gospel History and Its Transmission*, p. 256.

To judge the book as history is to condemn the author for not writing a different book.

The Synoptics are rich in indigenous information about the life and thought of the period in both the narrative and the teaching sections. The Fourth Gospel is interested in incident and circumstances only as back-drops to the theological ideology the book so consistently propagates. The conclusion is inescapable that it was compiled with this end in view (as indeed it plainly states) and the compiler, as Origen realised, did not hesitate to subordinate every other interest to this purpose, including historical verisimilitude.

The book's considerable literary qualities, narrative power, skill in dialogue, use of repetition, tone of high seriousness, are all fused to the great end of passionate persuasion. If it has had a unique place in Christian tradition, as it undoubtedly has, it is not because it gives a credible portrait of a Jesus who lived, taught and died in the Palestine of the late Jewish apocalyptic, but because it does not. Its historical unreality contributes to the reasons why it has been valued—a religious and theological masterpiece certainly, but not a document to be regarded as a primary historical authority in whole or in part.

Chapter Thirteen

Post-Synoptic questions

The main differences between the Synoptics and the Fourth Gospel used to be attributed to the fact that whereas they were the result of transmission of memories of what Jesus had said and done, it was in essence the account of an eye-witness who was able to report the inside story. This in part accounts for the reverence in which the Fourth Gospel has been held ever since it surmounted the initial prejudice against its acceptance into the canon.

The gospel itself gave ample encouragement to this view of its origin. It reported deeds and speeches which were unknown to the Synoptics. It suggested by an oddly naive kind of subtlety that not only was it authoritative but its ultimate source was the special confidant of Jesus, than whom no one was better able to transmit and interpret the essence of Jesus' life and thought.

We are now in a position to regard this kind of self-authentication with some doubt. Letters which reiterate that they are written by Paul excite our suspicion. We surmise that we are being led by the nose and the likelihood is that we are being led up the garden path.

If we can no longer accept the traditional explanation of the differences between the Synoptics and the Fourth Gospel, we must reassess them and consider alternatives. What are the reasons for the differences if they are not those between second-hand and first-hand reports? How does it come about that the Fourth Gospel is written in a way that gives the impression of eye-witness testimony? How does this affect our assessment of the worth of the book?

We begin from the fact that there is a difference in genre

between the Synoptics and the Fourth Gospel once we look beyond the superficial circumstance that they are both gospels in form, i.e. books dealing with the salient events in the life of Jesus. The primary distinction here is that between collection and composition, between transmission of existing material and creation of new material, between conservation of what is old and invention of something new.

Mark's gospel is essentially an assemblage of existing material about Jesus. True, it is not merely a record of things which he actually said and did. In transmission the material has been coloured by the beliefs of those through whom it has been handed on and at some points the facts have been misrepresented. But the intention is simple and the execution is naive. It is the work of a believer who is a compiler and who makes no pretentions to literary, creative or even expository ability.

The material itself has provided the obvious order in which it should be reproduced, the minimum of order for a document which must have a beginning, middle and end. It begins with the baptism, ends with the passion and everything else must find a place in between. Scholars are persuaded that the material in the middle is not in chronological order and have discovered no other order. Comment and transition notes are reduced to a minimum and for the most part one bare report of an incident follows another.

When we turn to Matthew and Luke we find that their gospels are more elegant in some respects but they are doing the same job. They each try to improve on the style of Mark. Matthew makes a more systematic arrangement of the middle material and Luke tries to produce a historical account that will approve itself to Hellenistic readers. But in effect they do over again the job done by Mark (with some additions), reporting what is handed down about Jesus.

Where they depart from this plan by elaboration, they

show themselves less trustworthy than in the rest of their writing. Each adds a new beginning. In both cases it includes a doubtful genealogy and a legendary birth-story. At the other end they add material on resurrection appearances which is secondary in quality. But none of the new material is presumed to be their own invention. It is traditional information which may have been garnered from oral or written sources of varying validity. They regard themselves as doing a job of reporting in the best way they can.

Now the Fourth Gospel is not a collection of information about Jesus in the synoptic sense. The compiler is not doing over and doing better the job that was done by Mark. What the Fourth Gospel Jesus does and says, for the most part was not seen or heard by anyone, even if this was later believed to be the case. Whatever the compiler believed about his material or would have liked his readers to believe, the composer knew he was not doing what Mark had done. He was not reporting the deeds and sayings of Jesus who became the focus of messianic expectations and the martyr to a historical cause in Palestine in the time of Pontius Pilate.

The Jesus of the Fourth Gospel is the protagonist in a cosmic drama, larger than historical life, a theophanic being who first came down from heaven before he ascended up to heaven and whose words and deeds were evidence of his divine sonship. One might say the synoptic material (or rather the little of it which he requires) becomes the scenery for the Fourth Gospel drama. The protagonist descended on Palestine in the first century as the most suitable place and time for him to touch earth. Essentially he is not of earth and not of time.

It might seem as if all he had in common with the subject of the Synoptics is the name Jesus and the fact of death by crucifixion. Other instances of apparent congruity are translated to a new climate. Even the crucifixion is not a sacrifice, a ransom for many, but exaltation of this being to that realm from which he came forth.

If we ask why the Fourth Gospel should be written in this fashion and not after the pattern of the Synoptics, the answer cannot possibly be that the author had more, and more historical, information than the synoptic writers. (It is very doubtful if it could be that the compiler thought his material was really more of the same kind as theirs.) Fundamentally it was because his view of the meaning of the Christian faith was different from, and to his own mind superior to, that in the Synoptics. This in turn meant that there was a difference in his view of Jesus and his significance. The gospel according to him is Jesus himself. He is the way, the truth and the life.

There is a natural development here irrespective of whether it is regarded as an essential development. If we begin from the notion that the gospel (good news) is the word which Jesus spoke, namely, that the kingdom of God is at hand, we proceed to the next stage that the gospel is the word about Jesus, his death, resurrection and coming, and hence by a less easy transition to the thought that the gospel is Jesus himself as the object of trust and hope.

This, however, does not account for the kind of transformation of Jesus which takes place in the Fourth Gospel. We know that believers in Jesus continued well into the second century to regard him more or less as the Synoptic writers did and opposed the teaching of the Fourth Gospel when it first appeared. In the latter part of the second century the church fiercely opposed the extension of ideas latent in the Fourth Gospel and branded them as Gnostic heresy.

What this means in effect is that it is possible to see how Jesus of Nazareth could come to be regarded as the Jewish Messiah by Jews and thence as the Christian Messiah by believers who formed a Jewish-Gentile Christian church. But how is the transition made from this to the notion of Jesus as temporary incarnation of the divine unless the idea of incarnation is forcibly brought into association with the Christian belief from outside the original tradition?

In the Prologue is the answer to this question. For the Logos to become flesh, the Logos must exist. For the Logos to become flesh in Jesus, Jesus must exist. The marriage of these two is the creative act and the commanding thought in the mind of the writer, whether he himself is the originator or simply a member of a school.

Once equate Jesus with the Word (however you come to conclude that the Word can indeed become flesh and has done so), then the process of glorification is a natural sequence, just as natural as the conclusion of the Synoptics, for instance, that since Jesus is undoubtedly the Messiah, he must have made a messianic entry into Jerusalem. The Fourth Gospel is then in some respect a work of the creative imagination on the subject of what God would be like in human form. The Prologue bypasses the question of how he enters the world, and the crucifixion and resurrection answer the question of how he accomplishes his exodus and returns to the Father.

In the period in which the Fourth Gospel was produced, all ingredients for this creative construction are present. But its accomplishment remains one of the major feats of the human spirit. It was, to take one signal instance, the teaching that the Word became flesh that struck Augustine with the force of revelation. He knew of the Word. He knew of the flesh. But the Word becoming flesh was the genius of Christianity.

If we turn to the position which this gospel has occupied as a theological document, there are two errors to be avoided. The temptations are to underestimate or to overestimate its originality. The first is the mistake of those who see the development of Christian doctrine as an inevitable, uniform progressive appreciation of the truth of Christianity up to its final formulation in the historic creeds. The second is congenial to those who are impressed by the part played by the great minds that give direction to theological thought and justify our speaking, for example, of Pauline, Augustinian or Barthian theology.

Enough has been said to support the argument that the Fourth Gospel is not simply the natural result of meditation on the meaning of the historical life of Jesus by a mind capable of drawing out the full implications of that event. The gospel is one of the latest books in the New Testament. This does not carry with it the implication that its theology is the inevitable consummation of New Testament theology, subsuming, completing and growing out of all that went before. 'The word became flesh' cannot be excogitated from Paul or Mark. The notion that the Christological debates leading to the orthodox creed are the result of divine inevitability is what H. von Camphausen calls 'the fiction of unbroken uniformity'. While the Fourth Gospel has a unique part to play in the process which in fact led to Chalcedon and beyond, the process itself partook of the nature of historical development.

On the other hand, to see this document as an inexplicable surd, an unexpected outcrop in an otherwise uniform landscape, is also mistaken. There is evidence that the marriage of Logos ideas with the gospel message was only to be expected in that age of syncretism.

'The general theological tone of the gospel was characteristic of a number of writers who did not acquire it from the Fourth Gospel', is the judgment of J. N. Saunders[1]. He cites Justin, Ignatius, Polycarp and possibly the writers of Barnabas, Hermas, and Diognetus. M. F. Wiles[2] thinks that, though Tatian and Theophilus refer to the Prologue of the Fourth Gospel, probably 'the real derivation of their thought

[1]   J. N. Saunders, *The Fourth Gospel in the Early Church.*
[2]   M. F. Wiles, *The Spiritual Gospel*, p. 99.

is independent, and they were simply attempting to link up their own conceptions with similar ideas in the Fourth Gospel, whose prestige and recognition as an authoritative scripture was steadily growing'.

Here we may have a clue to the kind of originality which can be attributed to the Fourth Gospel and the kind of influence it certainly exerted in the second and subsequent centuries. As far as we know, this is the first book which propagated the fertile interaction between the Logos idea and the Christian message in gospel form. It was probably the only book which did so in a manner which was not repulsive to the measure of historical concern which is present in the Synoptic Gospel tradition.

This was a daring project which ultimately succeeded. It cashed in on the popularity which gospel books already in existence were rapidly acquiring in the churches. The Pauline Corpus may not yet have been in existence and in any case epistles could never have the kind of influence which was inevitably reserved for those books which authoritatively recounted the words and deeds of the Lord. Once the Fourth Gospel was accepted into that category, a gospel written by an apostle, its theological prestige was inevitable.

Who was responsible for this stroke of genius? It would appear from the analysis that the book was the work of a compiler who himself compounded a document which gave distinctive treatment to the traditional outline of events, with additional material, partly relating to a Jerusalem ministry and partly private instruction to the disciples. A poem from another source was adapted as introduction and the whole furnished with concluding verses which contributed to the acceptance of the gospel as an authoritative document.

What this accomplished was the success of the kind of thinking about the gospel which made it triumphant in the Graeco-Roman world. It is justified by its fruits. It is the outreach of this document as a rethinking of the nature and destiny of man in the light of the potent conceptions of its day which will remain valuable, rather than the formal creed to which its basic doctrine gives rise.

E. F. Scott[3], writing of this gospel said, 'the purely religious view is overlaid or obscured by the conception of Christianity as a speculative system which makes its primary appeal to the logical intelligence'. The whole history of the Fourth Gospel in Christian theology and Christian devotion belies this statement. The gospel is the triumph of 'the purely religious view' over both the speculative systems of gnosticism and the traditional historical view of Jewish Christianity.

If it did not displace, it at least greatly modified the materialist, traditionalist Christianity which would have confined Jesus' message and religion to a new form of Judaism, incapable of captivating the world of western culture. Ideas of Jesus bounded by history and tradition, ideas of the kingdom of God and the second coming confined within Jewish apocalyptic moulds, ideas of the sacraments incapable of spiritualisation, ideas of the cross and resurrection restricted to sacrifice and revivification, would have doomed the new faith to early extinction. The Fourth Gospel was concerned that it should be spirit and life, let loose in the world as a power for new birth.

Similarly, the speculative systems of the second century with their appeal to snob intellectualism were capable only of breeding leaders who could not hope to have followers, an army without common soldiers. The Fourth Gospel is concerned to stress the reality of life and the possibility of new life. However tenuous its hold on past history, the reality of the incarnation is central to its teaching.

To some extent it took for granted and used the recital of the tradition about Jesus' life as reflected in the Synoptic Gospels. But the very fact that the Logos and Jesus are one

[3] E. F. Scott, *The Fourth Gospel*, p. 98.

in the Fourth Gospel is sufficient to show that that writer has
no merely speculative intention, however boldly his own
imagination works once the identification is made. Like Paul
he wants no other gospel. Redemption is by Jesus and it is a
present reality, not merely a future hope or an intellectual
enigma.

A striking feature of the Fourth Gospel is the extent to
which it is concerned with the present (i.e. post-crucifixion)
relation between Jesus and those who believe in him. The
Synoptics plainly relate what Jesus did and said while he
was on earth and only in the closing stages of *Matthew* and
Luke do they refer at all to the implications of the belief in
his resurrection, namely that Jesus is with his disciples
always (Matthew 28.20 specifically).

The Fourth Gospel on the other hand in its central portion
expounds an intimate, present and personal association
between Jesus and those who are believing in him at the time
when the gospel is being written and read. In other words
the Jesus who speaks is not a figure out of the past but the
ever-living Lord. To this extent we may say that a portion of
this Fourth Gospel is not, strictly speaking, gospel in the
same sense as the Synoptics are. The book is ostensibly in
gospel form but a large part of it is hortatory and epexegetic
rather than narrative and descriptive.

It is undoubtedly this feature which has given the Fourth
Gospel its paramount place in the devotional life of the
Church through the centuries. The emphasis is on Jesus in
the continuing present of the Church's life, on the immediacy
and efficacy of what he is to those who believe in him in
whatever historical period they may happen to live.

Jesus is the giver of living water and the believer who
drinks, in any age, will never thirst again (Chapter 4). He is
the bread of life and he who eats, no matter where or when,
will never hunger (Chapter 6). The story of the man born
blind (Chapter 9) is not merely the record of a historical

event. By implication it states that Jesus opens men's eyes, not only in Palestine and not only in that period when to believe in him meant being thrown out of the synagogue, but always. Jesus is the good shepherd who lays down his life for his sheep and has other sheep (besides those in the past and present) who will hear his voice (Chapter 10). He raised Lazarus and is now the resurrection and the life so that whoever believes will never perish (Chapter 11). Because Jesus lives, believers will live also and Jesus and the Father will come and live with them (Chapter 14). Jesus is the vine giving life to the branches (Chapter 15). Believers in every age abide in him and he in them. The Paraclete (Chapter 16) is his *alter ego* so that after his bodily presence is removed, his spiritual presence more than compensates. Jesus prays for his own who are in the world, not only for those now living but for those who will believe in him in the future (Chapter 17).

This method of indicating the implications of the Christian faith for his own day is not likely to be an invention of the writer. It is the method of the Old Testament prophet when he says: 'Thus saith the Lord'. Hebrew has no way of expressing the inward thoughts of a man without using direct speech. 'He said within himself' followed by *oratio recta* is equivalent to our "He thought that" followed by *oratio obliqua*.

Thus the prophet Isaiah does not write, 'This is what I think the will of God is for us, that we mustn't think sacrifices are a substitute for obedience to his will'. He writes: 'To what purpose is the multitude of your sacrifices unto me? saith the Lord' (Isaiah 1.11). Similarly the author of the Apocalypse, writing of his own conception of the significance of Jesus, says that he heard a great voice saying, 'I am Alpha and Omega' (*Revelation* 1.11). It is not implied that this was the echo of something actually said by Jesus at a particular period in his earthly ministry. This is a method of expressing the instant apprehension of what the Church ought to know and believe at that moment of writing.

We may be sure that we are not dealing here with a phenomenon of isolated instances but with the common practice of the 'prophets' of the early church. The dangers of this practice are, of course, obvious. It was necessary to issue warnings against the consequences of abuse, as for example, that the church must 'try the spirits whether they are of God: because many false prophets are gone out into the world' (1 John 4.1). The Church of the second century yearned for confirmatory revelations and the most obvious guarantee that could be offered by those who ministered to this avid desire was in the form, 'I tell you, Jesus says . . .'.

The broadest distinction between the teacher of the Law and the prophet in the Old Testament era was that the one referred to a word given once for all by God in old time— 'God said . . .' and the other to the word for his own day— 'Thus saith the Lord . . .'. No doubt the same distinction was present in the time we are concerned with. There were those who taught on the basis of what was reported as the teaching of Jesus in the days of his flesh and those who made ecstatic announcements of up-to-date revelation in the direct speech of the present tense.

The Fourth Gospel is unique in that it is an amalgam of the two in the guise of the former. The 'Jesus said' in parts of the Gospel is equivalent to 'Jesus says today'. The distinction was one that would be readily appreciated and it is unrealistic to imagine that every time a second-century writer employed the formula, 'Jesus said', he was infallibly referring to the historical words of Jesus during his lifetime.

This direct speech element which has reference to the relation between Jesus and the second-century believer we shall call the 'non-gospel' portions of the Fourth Gospel. They are the writer's thoughts about what Jesus is saying to the church of his own time and in this instance they reiterate the message, that Jesus is the ever-present Lord and giver of life, the unique Son of the Father who is the only way to the Father, that the most important element in the Christian experience is the relation of the believer to the object of his faith and that object is nothing other than this living Jesus.

The ardour and singleness of purpose with which the writer pursued this intention probably indicates the intensity of his conviction, as does the very direct fashion in which he chose to express it. It is as if nothing but the word of Jesus himself could convey the strength of his certitude and the cardinal import of the truth itself.

By this formula, 'Jesus said', it is evident then that he is not insisting on the historicity of *ipsissima verba* of Jesus of Nazareth. On the contrary, it is the fact of Jesus' intimate relation to the believer not the form that he emphasises. The words of Jesus are spirit and life because they are not past and what the believer hears is not merely an echo from the past.

For this writer the Christian life is not learning what Jesus said and did in Palestine but believing and obeying the present word of Jesus from day to day. That word is new every morning in its dynamic and creative effect. The light of it does not shine from first-century Palestine as if it were the dying gleam from a receding beacon. It shone then and there but it shines now and here with the same instant majesty. The truth of it is not being shrouded by the mists of time. It is truth for today, as believers are able to receive it.

This feature has so large a place in the document (to the exclusion of the actual deeds and words of Jesus which must have been known to the writer and compiler and which form the essence of the normal gospel) that we are almost bound to conclude, firstly, that it was the original inspiration which forms the dynamic of the book, and, secondly, that there is a polemic purpose at the heart of it. If these 'non-gospel' portions are a separate source, it is not improbable that the

rest of the document was used to form a casket or a vehicle
for it. The whole was given the semblance of a gospel in the
belief that this was the best way to preserve and to propagate
the particular emphasis of the 'non-gospel' portion. This
book was not written to supersede or replace the other
gospels (i.e. books largely dealing with the historical facts of
the life and teaching of Jesus). It was given gospel form
because this was one of the two established types of Christian literature in vogue at the time.

It seems that anyone who had anything important to com-
municate to the Church in written form in the second century
was more than likely to send it forth in the form of a gospel
or in the form of letters. The many apocryphal gospels and
the number of series of letters that entered circulation in
that era can only reflect the belief that these were the author-
ised literary genera, used and sanctified by apostles and
apostolic men. This being so, it is obvious that a document
which centred on the relation between Jesus and his own
should appear in gospel form.

The emphatic way in which the central conviction per-
meates the 'non-gospel' sections of the gospel and the
confident vehemence with which it is expressed betray an
apologetic intention, a consciousness of the utter rightness
of the conviction and also the awareness that it is not assured
of automatic acceptance with a wider public.

In form it is a dogmatic reiteration by means of many
metaphors of a truth which brooks no contradiction. Jesus is
living water, bread from heaven, sight to the blind, the door,
the good shepherd, the resurrection and the life, to those who
believe. Not to believe is to thirst, hunger, be blind, the prey
of robbers, dead.

This categorical strain which centres on 'believing' has
made this document more than any other in the New Testament responsible for the dogmatic, heresy-hunting mentality
which was a recurrent feature of Church history. It has

seemed to give sanction to an anti-Christian attitude to the whole Jewish nation and it is not possible to exonerate the gospel as a whole from this charge. But it has also given impetus to doctrinal schism through its apparent emphasis on the primacy of belief.

In this respect, however, the inference is surely mistaken. The Fourth Gospel does not emphasise the intellectual content of belief but the total experience of conviction. It is true that the incessant stress on believing which is found in the gospel makes it inevitable that, once the disposition is present to emphasise content rather than experience, the gospel becomes an authority for dogmatism. This result came about because in one respect the gospel was only too successful, the fault of successive generations rather than of the originators of the work.

It is reckoned that this gospel uses the verb *pisteuein* with about nine times the frequency of other gospels but never once uses the noun *pistis*. Assent to some intellectual formulation of faith is far from encompassing the writer's intention. What he means by 'believing' is 'having an invincible conviction that goes to the depths of the personality'. For him it is the conviction that is fundamental, not the terms in which it may be inadequately put into words. This is why he uses personal direct speech.

The essence of being a Christian is not believing certain traditional statements of Jesus or about Jesus but believing in Jesus himself. It is one thing to believe that Jesus gave living water when he was in Palestine and another to drink the living water which Jesus now gives. The writer's stress is on the present experience of drinking, eating, seeing, abiding, living, the whole man actively engaged in total relationship to a divine presence.

It has already been suggested that in the manner and method of this communication there is an awareness that the place of priority he wishes it to have in the Church was not likely to be granted automatically. The writer is not flogging a dead horse; he is breaking new ground. We must try, therefore, to envisage the circumstances in which this gospel was published and what it was intended to achieve, and this will occupy us shortly.

Meantime we note that the apologetic attitude of the Fourth Gospel is not confined to the passages we have called 'non-gospel'. It has long been recognised that there is a polemical attitude to the Jews, to the followers of the Baptist, to gnosticism or incipient gnosticism, although it is possible to overstate this last as far as the gospel (as distinct from the Epistles) is concerned.

But when we consider these three subjects we find that they do not answer to the kind of situation which the passages we have in mind deal with. The theme of personal union between Jesus and His own is not directly the point at issue between the Church and any of these external opponents.

The polemic against the Jews reaches its climax in 6.32-59. The issue is the relation between Jesus and God. They oppose Jesus because 'He makes Himself equal with God'. Now the answer to this charge requires a theological disquisition on the nature of God and the nature of Jesus and the connection between the two: this we do not find in these passages. It is only obliquely that the relation between Jesus and believers could figure in this contest. Even so, this relation would have to be treated in theological rather than in experiential terms, if it were to serve the purpose.

Similarly, any references to the Baptist's followers implied in the Fourth Gospel turn on a different subject, namely, the relation between Jesus and John the Baptist as regards Messiahship and priority. John himself is made to testify that Jesus is the Christ, the one who, as he himself had testified, takes precedence 'because he was before me'. This subject is not touched in what we have called the 'non-gospel' passages.

Again, regarding gnostic tendencies the issues are the reality of the life and death of Jesus, the primacy of the Logos in creation, the nature of divine sonship and the like, all themes separate from that of the meaning of Jesus (in the Fourth Gospel sense) for his own disciples.

It seems that the situation in mind as far as the 'non-gospel' theme is concerned is not outside the Christian body but within. The writer is saying something to the Church in its nature and not with reference to outside and antagonistic elements. He is intending to some extent to bring to Christians a fresh (not necessarily entirely new) vision of what they are as members of the Christian Church. He is giving a fresh definition of what if means to be a Christian or bringing to the forefront what he considers to be the essence of Christian discipleship, possibly in view of the danger that it may be or already has been overlooked or overlaid within the Church itself.

If our reasoning so far holds good and if there is a conscious desire on the part of the writer of the 'non-gospel' portions to propagate a new emphasis within the Church, we must look in the same area for the emphasis which is to be dislodged from the prime place. That is to say, since he deals with the relation between Jesus and his own, he is in some respect at odds with the prevailing idea of that relation within the Church or in some churches at the time of writing.

We must therefore ask what view of the relation between Jesus and the second-century Christians could have been widespread which in essence was inimical or prejudicial to that set out by this writer. Since we can characterise the writer's view as dynamic, present, direct, intimate, rooted in conviction, free and open for the future, is there present at his time a view that can be characterised as tied to the past, indirect, formal, legalistic, traditional, unfitted to face the future?

Broadly speaking, the Church in the second century was

immersed in a contention about its own identity in a new age. It had clearly differentiated itself from Judaism proper, both theologically and practically. The place that Christians gave to Jesus was not yet strictly defined in intellectual terms. There were varieties of opinion on such questions as pre-existence, the virgin-birth, when and how he became Messiah and how the title 'Son of God' was to be interpreted. Nevertheless belief in Jesus effectively distinguished Christians from Jews who gave the supreme place under God to Moses and the Law. In the empire it was being understood that Christians were not Jews and that Christianity was not therefore automatically to be regarded as a *religio licita*.

Within the Church itself, however, the need for some degree of uniformity of belief and practice was becoming insistent. This is the age in which the Church must come to some conclusion about the place of the Law and the Old Testament, about prophecy and the gifts of the spirit, about the relation of theology to Hellenistic thought.

These are some of the manifestations of the quest for identity. They are embodied in controversies regarding those who were the direct descendants of primitive Jewish Christianity on the one hand and the Marcionites on the other regarding apocalyptism and the prophetic movements which brought the Church into disrepute by their extravagances and regarding the docetic and gnostic types of thought represented by Cerinthus and Valentinus. We may sum up the situation by saying that tradition, experience and speculation are in competition for the first place in the scale of the Church's priorities and much depended on the outcome.

It was also, of course, an age of important developments in Church organisation and government, an age when the New Testament canon was being formed, an age of struggle with and suffering at the hands of the state. These, however are matters beyond our immediate concern. The question we ask is, How does the Fourth Gospel, and in particular the 'non-gospel' material, fit into such a period? What contribution does it make to the Church's quest for identity? The answer, it seems, must be that its weight is not on the side of the traditional, very much on the side of experience and, if we are thinking of the gospel as a whole, to some considerable extent on the side of intellectual adventurousness.

To take the last of these three statements, it seems incontrovertible that the Fourth Gospel in the second century was seen by some as gnostic in tendency. This is apparent in the fact that the first known commentary on this gospel is that of Heracleon, a Valentinian gnostic who wrote about 170 A.D. Contrariwise, it was rejected by others who were particularly opposed to the logos doctrine and are known as Alogi. They attributed the gospel to the (gnostic) heretic Cerinthus.

We are not concerned here with the question how far the Fourth Gospel is gnostic in tendency and to what extent it contributed to the growing popularity of the type of thought already present in the writings of Justin, Ignatius, Polycarp and others. Our interest is in trying to discover why and to what extent it was felt necessary to bring to the forefront, in so insistent and dogmatic a manner, the pragmatic factor of the personal presence of Jesus with his own, and what kind of notion of that relation would be displaced or demoted if this point of view should prove triumphant.

For this reason the opponents of the Fourth Gospel are more important to the present study than the tendencies which might be favourable to its acceptance as authoritative. The opponents are in fact those who hold to the traditional view of Jesus. To them the Fourth Gospel was a break with the hallowed past, an innovation, and was opposed on these grounds. As a gospel it did not square with those already in circulation and did not present the accredited picture of Jesus as regarded either his status or his life. The logos doctrine did not belong to the original belief of the church and the chronology of the life and substance of the teaching did not agree with the synoptic type of account.

From the traditional point of view these criticisms were unanswerable. But the compilers of the Fourth Gospel were evidently prepared to override this fact. Something other than strict regard for the primitive form of belief took priority in their thinking. On this view the answer to the question, What is a Christian? was not, 'One who holds to the early conception of Jesus and waits for his return in power'. The crux of the matter lay in emphasising the experience of the living presence of Jesus here and now. In other words, the past was not regarded as sacrosanct and determinative of the future of the Christian religion for all time to come. In essence the Christian faith is a living and creative experience in the present, not only a memory of things past and a hope for things to come.

From another angle we may say that certainly the author of the 'non-gospel' material and most likely also the compiler of the Fourth Gospel as a whole were standing for Christian liberty in their own age as the apostle Paul did in his. But whereas in the Pauline letters it is liberty from legalism, in the Fourth Gospel it is traditionalism that is regarded as the restraining influence. In the one case it was freedom from Judaism, in the other freedom from the swaddling bands of early Christianity itself. Having dissociated itself from the restrictions of the Mosaic tradition, Christianity must now dissociate itself from the restrictive tradition of its own creation if it was to live and grow in a new age and enjoy a vital future.

That this was the situation in which the Fourth Gospel appeared can be appreciated if we consider what that early tradition was and why it could be regarded as restrictive in the second century. We are dealing with a period in which it was still not doctrinally settled as to how Jesus should be regarded by his followers. The earliest views were to be found alongside those which were tending in the direction of the definition later vitrified in the creeds of the fourth and fifth centuries.

Christianity took its rise from the belief that Jesus was his people's Messiah. After his crucifixion it was believed he would come again and establish the Messianic kingdom. The proof that he was Messiah—as distinct from the belief that he would be Messiah—was to be his return in power and glory, which was the vivid expectation of the primitive Christian society.

That same future event, the parousia, was to be the final demonstration that Jesus was risen, for his Messiahship was not essentially a secret to be known only by a chosen few but the manifestation of the power of God to all the world. The glory of the Lord would be revealed and all flesh would see it together. Faith would give place to sight very soon.

The primitive Church believed that Jesus was risen, on the testimony of the few who were convinced that he would come again. There was no need at the time to require objective proof. The faith that the eagerly-awaited event would occur was self-sufficient. It was enough for Paul to state that others had seen Jesus after his death and that he himself had met him on the road to Damascus (there being no obvious distinction between the two sets of events). His converts were not required to have first hand evidence of the resurrection but only to believe the apostolic testimony. In other words, they were not expected to say, 'Show us the same evidence that you have seen'. It was enough to believe that shortly the proof would be evident to everybody.

Only when this proof, in the form of the parousia, was not forthcoming, did the Church begin to doubt whether the end of the age was indeed imminent and to require more evidence of the resurrection and Messiahship of Jesus than the emphasis on final and imminent vindication had previously allowed them to think sufficient.

At this point two things were bound to happen. Firstly, the proof which was thought to be forthcoming almost immediately, was tending to become the substance of a hope that the believer at death would be united with Jesus and, consentaneously, the Messianic kingdom idea was ultimately to be displaced by the idea of the Church as a continuing institution whose members were guaranteed a blessed immortality at death. The sacraments were to become the means to this—'the medicine of immortality'.

Secondly, the resurrection of Jesus had to be believed in without the expectation that proof would be provided by an impending parousia. Thus the resurrection became a crucial factor on its own account. Without it, belief in union with Jesus after death was felt to be void and the faith that Jesus was Messiah lacked any practical foundation.

In consequence there is a need for more objective evidence that Jesus had indeed risen from the dead. This need is supplied by the provision of factual stories of bodily encounters with Jesus after his death. These purport to give proof that he is risen as distinct from merely inculcating the belief that he will come back at some future time.

It is noticeable that these stories, some of which are included in the closing chapters of Matthew and Luke, take on the kind of attendant circumstances that might be expected to belong to the originally expected proof of the resurrection and Messiahship of Jesus, the parousia. They are endowed with attributes that were associated with the return in glory, such as earth tremors and opening graves, accompanying angels, sudden, mysterious and awe-inspiring apparitions, meals symbolic of the Messianic banquet.

The apologetic of Christianity now depends on the belief that Jesus rose on the third day and that objective proof of this existed. The emphasis has moved from what was originally the climax of Messianic expectation, the return, to an event which is already past, an actual resurrection of

Jesus three days after crucifixion. This is the position at the beginning of the post-apostolic age to which most of the New Testament literature except the genuine Pauline letters seems to belong and in which it is fairly clearly to be discerned.

In these circumstances the Church is gradually being forced into a hopelessly excruciating situation, and that in regard to the cardinal factors of conviction and belief. It is on the rack between a receding point in past history, namely, the crucifixion and resurrection of Jesus, and a receding point in the future, namely, the end of the world.

The believer's relation to Jesus in these conditions was bound to appear to be less and less immediate and personal. Remorselessly he was being borne further and further away from the twin points of his faith and it must be remembered that the idea of Messiah carried with it no inbuilt doctrine of a present and personal union between him and those he would ultimately save. During the interim between the crucifixion and the parousia he is in heaven.

The posture of the primitive Church was that of waiting for his return. Even the theology of Paul based on the idea that the last days have proleptically begun, did not get beyond the idea of being in Christ in the sense of being one of those who are being prepared to enjoy the blessings of the new age and who meantime are given the spirit as the 'earnest' or 'pledge' or 'first-fruits' of what is eagerly awaited.

When the writers of the second and third centuries describe the Christology of those who are now regarded as heretics because the logos Christology was now becoming triumphant, it is evident that they are describing the primitive Christology which has survived to their own time. Justin[4], about the middle of the second century, spoke against those who see Jesus as simply a man, *anthrōpos ex anthrōpōn genomenon*, who became Messiah by election and

[4] Justin Martyr, *Dialogue c. Trypho*, 47, 48.

choice; Irenaeus[5], writing towards the end of the same century, tells us of those who deny the virgin-birth; while Origen[6], in the mid-third century, is of the opinion that some so-called Christians differ little from Jews. We cannot doubt that this condemned pattern of belief belongs to those who were doggedly conserving the earliest form of the Christian faith when all that distinguished Christianity from Judaism was the fact that Christians believed they knew who Messiah would be, Jesus, now in heaven, soon to come in glory.

But those who were determined to be true to the origins of their faith were at the same time being deprived of the dynamic which it originally provided. The mere passage of time was proving to be enervating. The expected kingdom receded into the future and the link with the historic circumstances which gave rise to the conviction that it was Jesus who was to be Messiah became progressively more tenuous. Jesus remained the object of their faith, but history and the elusiveness of the parousia were reducing faith to a form of faithfulness to a tradition, and Jesus to the status of a second Moses whose words and deeds were revered but whose presence was not immediate.

Now it ought to be made clear that the argument is not that this was what happened to the Church at the beginning of the second century, only that in some instances this was the position and that (and this is very much to the point), if a purely historical and traditional answer were to be given to the question facing the Church in its search for identity, this would be the effect of it, loss of vitality. Ebionism was the extreme instance of this calamity. It was fossilized early Christianity. If the origins of the movement were to be the criteria which settled the question about what the true Church was and what it should believe in the second century, then the effect was bound to be a living death for the

---

5 Irenaeus, *adv. Haer*, 1.22.
6 Origen, *De Princip*. IV. 1.

Christian faith. The Fourth Gospel offers a more excellent way.

It is reasonable to suppose that the Fourth Gospel attained its position in the canon and its influence on the Church's theology because it was seen to offer answers or better answers to questions which the Synoptic tradition and primitive belief either left unanswered or did not answer in a way which was adequate to the needs of a different age. It provided a theology which was recognised in due course as preferable for a variety of reasons to that of the Synoptics but yet could be considered not incompatible therewith, and a rationale of the Christian life which was not tied to the milieu of the era of late Jewish apocalyptic. In short, the Fourth Gospel supplied the Church with the possibility of an ageless theology and an ageless explication of Christian experience.

The doubts and fears of the age fastened on the most important convictions bequeathed from the initial period of the Church's life. Epiphanius[7], for example, states that even in apostolic times a form of Christianity was in vogue in Asia Minor which held that Christ's resurrection had not yet taken place and would occur only as the inception of the general resurrection of the dead. Ignatius[8] also speaks of the same notion.

The argument seems to have been that the resurrection of Jesus could not be separated from the introduction of the new age through his parousia, all three being considered as constituents of one divine event. The parousia and the new age have not yet arrived, ergo Christ has not been raised. The Synoptic Gospels provided no kind of relief for the tension of such a situation. Hence the longing for some new revelation which would confirm the Church's faith and deal with the hiatus between the resurrection of Jesus and the

[7] Epiphanius, *Haer.* XXVIII, 6.1.4.
[8] Ignatius, *Ad. Eph.* 20.1.

expected consummation. If Jesus has been raised, why has the parousia not occurred? What has happened to the promised programme? Has the Church misconstrued the divine intention?

The evidence of this frame of mind lies in the literature which was produced in response to it. This literature purported to derive its authority from Jesus himself through his apostles. It comprised teaching given under the form of revelation made privately to the disciples by Jesus either before his crucifixion of after his resurrection. For example, *Epistula Apostolorum*, dating from the middle of the second century, purports to be an encyclical sent out by the eleven disciples after the resurrection. It records conversations between the apostles and the risen Christ and probably comes from Asia Minor. From the early second century we have the *Apocalypse of Peter* which gives an account of addresses given to the disciples on the Mount of Olives with portents of his second coming and the end of the world. The persistence of this type of literature is seen in the *Didascalia Apostolorum* which seems to have come from North Syria in the early third century under the title *The Catholic Teaching of the Twelve Apostles and Holy Disciples of our Redeemer*, and the *Pistis Sophia*, also from the third century, which records instructions given by Jesus to some of his disciples after his resurrection.

The Fourth Gospel, widely believed to have originated in Asia Minor, is perhaps best thought of as the finest example of this type of literature, literature which speaks in the words of Jesus himself to the needs of the Church in the post-Synoptic period. According to the Muratorian Fragment it was believed to have been written down by the apostle John as a result of a revelation given to Andrew and certified by all the apostles.

This gospel had the ability to give a new and liberating interpretation of the significance of Jesus which was welcome not only for its own sake but for the release it afforded from the tension which characterised the post-apostolic age. It ultimately came to be regarded as the best interpretation of the historical deeds recorded in the Synoptics (and was even thought by many to be preferable to them as a historical account of the events of Jesus' earthly life) and as the best solution of the problems that arose as a result of the hopes and promises which the Synoptic Gospels raised but left unfulfilled.

The Fourth Gospel achieved this pre-eminence by proclaiming an enhanced status for the Christ, the object of the Church's worship, which was not incompatible with the Hellenistic doctrine of the Logos as the divine agent in relation to the world and to the human race, although this is explicitly stated only in the Prologue (1.1-18). He was with God in the beginning as the agent in creation and became flesh for the salvation of those who believe in him. His divine mission did not start at his baptism (Mark) or at his birth (Matthew and Luke) but in the beginning, the absolute beginning of all things, in the bosom of the Father from whom he came forth. The characteristic definition of God in the Fourth Gospel is 'He who sent me' (Jesus) for the redemption of his people.

This exalted status altered every other aspect of his relation to those who believe in him, including the meaning the Church had attached to resurrection, parousia and the end of the age.

The resurrection of Jesus is neither denied nor postponed but given a new significance as the guarantee of who Jesus is (the one who comes from and returns to the Father, cf. 20.17) and what he does for those who believe in him (gives them eternal life now, cf. 10.27, 28). Those who have not seen the risen Christ but yet believe are blessed (20.29). While in the Synoptics the resurrection is the vindication of his life and message as a prophet mighty in word and deed, and the source of the expectation that he will come again in power, in the Fourth Gospel it is the return to the Father whence he came which issues in the gift of the Spirit and the assurance of his continual presence with his disciples. The conclusion to Matthew's gospel belongs to the type of literature we have been considering since it records the words of the risen Christ about the future and conveys the same assurance about the presence of Jesus with his disciples as John 14-17. But there it is qualified with the words *heōs tēs sunteleias tou aiōnos*, till the end of the (present) age, or, as an earlier document has it, *achri hou elthē*, till he comes (I *Corinthians* 11.26).

With regard to the parousia, once again it is neither denied nor postponed but is displaced in importance by the emphasis on the presence of Christ, on the Holy Spirit and on judgment here and now rather than at the end of the age (3.18; 5.24). The favourite title used in *Mark*, for example, is Son of Man (14 occurrences) as compared with Son of God (4), Son of David (3) and the Son (1). Most of these refer to the future betrayal, crucifixion and coming in power and judgment at a future date. The favourite title in the Fourth Gospel is the Son (without qualification) which occurs seventeen times. There are thirteen occurrences of Son of Man, nine of Son of God and two of Son of David. The Son of Man sayings here refer to the (past) descent from heaven (3.13), the present and future glorification (12.23; 13.31), the lifting up or ascending to heaven (6.62; 8.28; 12.34). There is no reference whatever to the future descending in power. The glory resides in the person of Jesus now and it will be fully demonstrated when he is 'lifted up' and returns to the Father.

Clearly this is an important change of emphasis away from the apocalyptic expectation of a crisis due to the irruption of a supernatural agent at some imminent but indefinite moment in the future, to the actual and permanent status of one who is, was and will be the bearer of the glory which he has from his father eternally. It is interesting to note, nevertheless, that the Fourth Gospel alone of New Testament books reproduces the Hebrew title 'Messiah' (1.14; 4.25), and that the phrase *hē eschatē hēmera*, 'the last day', is found in this gospel only (6.29, 40, 54; 11.24; 12.48), though Macgregor[9] notes that the idea 'has little place in John's scheme of thought, according to which life and judgment alike are present and inward rather than future and dramatic'.

Wendt regarded this phrase ('the last day') as an interpolation and in this has been followed by many, including Bultmann. It may be so, but at which point in the evolution of the Gospel to its present form would be difficult to decide. Dodd[10] argued that the term 'Messiah' in this gospel must 'be stripped of a large part of its connotation in Jewish usage' and is to be understood 'only in the sense of authority in the spiritual sphere, the authority which belongs to one who knows and communicates absolute truth'.

Mention of the last day brings us to the conception of the new age and the contrast between the Synoptics and the Fourth Gospel in this respect. Bernard[11] commented, 'We find in the Fourth Gospel, on the one hand, phrases entirely in the manner, so to speak, of *Matthew* and of *Acts* and of Paul, as to Messiah and Messiah's judgment at the last; and, on the other hand, a wider and more catholic presentation of Jesus as the world's King and Saviour, whose kingdom is already established in some degree'. We might not express this juxtaposition in these terms, but obviously the movement is away from the early modes of thinking and the notion of a decisive event in the future. Thus 5.28, 29 is in the idiom of the Synoptic Gospels regarding resurrection to judgment as are these references we have noted to the events

9 G. H. C. Macgregor, *John*, p. 146.
10 C. H. Dodd, *The Interpretation of the Fourth Gospel*, pp. 88, 9.
11 J. H. Bernard, *St. John*, Vol. 1, p. CLVIII.

of the last day. But the weight of evidence is in favour of the notion of *zōē aiōnios* (eternal life) already present to those who believe. For them the judgment is not to come; they have already passed from death to life (3.15, 16, 36; 6.40, 47 also 4.23; 5.25; 11.25, 26; 9.39).

The incident of the raising of Lazarus in chapter 11 presents a significant confrontation between the two modes of thought where Martha represents the Jewish eschatological outlook but Jesus himself presents the new emphasis. To refer to Dodd[12] again: 'The evangelist agrees with popular Christianity that the believer will enter into eternal life at the general resurrection, but for him this is a truth of less importance than the fact that the believer already enjoys eternal life, and the former is a consequence of the latter'. This statement assumes that the gospel is homogeneous but it does make the point that the two modes of thinking are present in the document. That the relationship between the two is one of cause and effect is in line with Dodd's idea of realised eschatology but it would be true to say in terms of priority that 'the former is antecedent to the latter'.

The Fourth Gospel thus effectively reduces the tension caused by the hiatus between the resurrection and the events of the end. Whereas, as we have seen, some (in Asia Minor at least) argued that all these related circumstances, namely, the resurrection of Jesus, the parousia and the beginning of the new age, were still in the future, and others thought that part was past and part yet to come, the Fourth Gospel produces a theology which places the spiritual implications of these events effectively in the present. The word for 'now' (*nun*) occurs twenty-nine times in the Fourth Gospel as against three in *Mark*, four in *Matthew* and fourteen in *Luke*. The risen Christ is the one who has come to his disciples and by faith in him they have already passed from death into the life of the world to come. The document as it

[12] C. H. Dodd, *op. cit.* p. 148.

stands does not deny that there are future events but it defuses the anxiety about the nature and occasion of such events by concentrating on the exalted and eternal status of the one who is now and always the Son of the Father in whom the believer already possesses the blessing which he came to bring.

If we now turn to the practical theology of the Christian life or how Christians explain to themselves what being a Christian means and how this affected the way they tended to think and act as Christians, we can see that the post-apostolic and post-synoptic age required to adjust itself to a new situation, if only because the stress of continuing to maintain the old ways of thought was becoming increasingly unbearable. The basic fact was that the age of the apostles was past and the events of the end had still not arrived and to many seemed as far away as ever. Indeed, to an increasing number the time in which they lived was one of growing doubt. The resurrection of Jesus was far behind and receding while the parousia had sunk beyond the horizon of the future. Many Christians could no longer believe that the divine event to which the Church had looked forward from its inception would occur in their day. Some began to question whether indeed it would now take place in the fashion which they had originally believed it would take, or perhaps whether it would occur at all.

Thus for the most practical of reasons the theology of hope which characterised the period of late Jewish apocalyptic was increasingly unable to sustain the weight of anxiety which the non-occurrence of the events of the end imposed on it. Jesus rose in the past. He ascended into heaven where he waits the appointed hour (*Acts* 3.21). But the hour will not strike. What then in the meantime is the dynamic of the Christian life? Is it simply a belief in a past historical event and a hope of a future uncertain event, both becoming less vivid as the years pass? Yet the Christian

movement grows and the Christian life is lived. It is not only
a belief and a hope but a faith as it had always been, but this
faith must have a theology which is relevant to itself and
its own age and the emphasis must be less on history and
eschatology and more on the present reality of Christian
experience. This change in emphasis is one of the prominent
features of the Fourth Gospel and one reason for its ultimate
predominance.

If we now look at the three constituents of the new age
which the synoptic tradition bequeathed to the Church from
this point of view, we see that the Fourth Gospel modifies
the programme in the direction of personal experience. Belief
that a past event had occurred and hope of a future consummation are perfected in faith in an exalted Lord. Whereas
for the writer of *I Corinthians* the greatest of Christian
virtues is love, for the Fourth Gospel it is whatever unites
them to the eternal Son who is the resurrection and the
life, who will not leave them bereft (*orphanous*, 14.18) and
through whom they have already passed beyond judgment
into life.

The historical events of the life of Jesus in Palestine are
seen not as a tale that is told but as the embodiment of his
power to be in every age alpha and omega to his followers.
They are his word which is bread, water, healing, sight,
resurrection and life. That he is no longer bodily present as
he was with the apostles is not a deprivation; he is spiritually
present. His gifts to believers are not the less therefore but
the greater and are summed up in the presence of the Spirit
(*paraclētos*).

The Fourth Gospel seems to indicate that it is not for
Christians to say they believe in the resurrection because the
apostles have said Jesus rose on the third day. The resurrection is primarily a fact of experience, not of history,
though it is not to be denied as a fact of history. Indeed, the
materialistic evidence offered in the Fourth Gospel goes

beyond that given in the Synoptics. Thomas does not actually touch the risen Christ but the implication is that he could have done so. However, the main import of the gospel is not that Jesus was resurrected at a receding point in time but that he is the resurrection in his own person. There is to be no regret that Christians of the latter days have not seen the Lord as the apostles did. He himself pronounces the blessing on those who have not seen and yet have believed. The past can be allowed to drop into history without any sense of loss. He is not there; he is here. He is not then; he is now.

The same kind of resolution is evolved for the other extremity of the situation, the events of the future. We have seen that the parousia has little place in the document and that the end of the age has lost most of its eschatological import. This is because in personal experience the things that belong to the new age have already become a reality for the believer here and now. Already those who abide in him have all they can ask or desire and if they need anything in the future they have only to ask. What is still to come can be awaited with patience meanwhile.

It can therefore be seen that the Fourth Gospel is designed to meet the needs of a generation for whom the traditional interpretation of resurrection, parousia and the new age had become a strait-jacket both for theology and for the interpretation of Christian experience, that it did so by a doctrine which ascribed to Jesus a status which could not be further enhanced without simply equating him with God and which, once accepted could not be relinquished, and that in consequence the primary tenets regarding resurrection, parousia and the new age together took on a significance which raised their doctrinal importance out of the arena of anxious deliberation into the serenity of an abiding experience of unity with the eternal Son. Thenceforth the questions for theology would be of a different kind.

Chapter Fourteen

A tract for the times

The insistence on the centrality of present communion between Jesus and his own which characterised the 'non-gospel'
material in the Fourth Gospel, was bound to have certain
repercussions, particularly on those doctrines which depended on historical event for their significance. They are the
doctrines which are based on the key occurrences in the
historical life of Jesus and on the temporal elements in the
Church's teaching about the post-crucifixion events of resurrection, ascension and parousia.

But it is unlikely that the repercussions we anticipate
would take the form of outright abolition or denial of these
historical or expected events. The belief in the presence of
Jesus here and now through his Spirit, however vivid and
potent, does not involve disbelieving in his physical presence
in the past history which is the milieu of revelation. Indeed,
there is no evidence that the compiler of the Fourth Gospel
(who, we take it, was in sympathy with the central thesis of
the non-gospel material) wished to deny that Jesus was
born, was crucified and would return in future power and
glory.

On the contrary, the Fourth Gospel has no *raison d'être*
if the historical life and death of Jesus are in question. The
reality and truth of Jesus' existence at a time and place in
history are the fundamental premiss of the gospel as a whole
Ho logos sarx egeneto—the Word became flesh. Becoming
sarx meant a real body, real hunger, real suffering and real
death. But it is not the body, the *sarx*, that is the revelation
of the divine presence on earth. Nothing that Jesus felt or
experienced historically is the *doxa* (glory) which the dis-

202

ciples beheld. That is present in the word of Jesus and that word is his own presence, the object of the verb *pisteuein* (believe).

The fact is, therefore, that the old and the new are found together, not because there is no distinction between the history and the revelation but because they are both essential to the gospel and the question at issue is the relation in which they stand to each other. The Fourth Gospel is built around the thesis that the revelation takes precedence over the history and the presence of Jesus with his disciples now takes precedence over his historical presence then in Palestine. To this extent the Fourth Gospel is concerned with the priorities of faith in an age when the events of the incarnation are no longer immediate.

These two elements come into contact but not into open antagonism. The Fourth Gospel does not deny the traditional facts and the views associated with them, but at the same time it leaves no doubt that it has found a more excellent way of stating what is the order of priority for Christian faith in its own and every post-crucifixion age.

We find, therefore, that time and again the historical events are unmentioned (not denied) or given a somewhat different nuance. This is the obvious sign that a new direction is given to the expression of the traditional faith but without any intention to antagonise. No attack is being mounted from a base outside the ambit of the apostolic tradition. It is a movement of renovation from within.

If this is so, then two results follow as to the purpose of the Fourth Gospel. It is not a deliberate rewriting of the gospel from a gnostic or proto-gnostic point of view, however much it may be true that forms of expression are used which were congenial to Hellenistic as opposed to Judaic types of thought. The urge to give a new form to the way in which Christianity is to be interpreted and expressed arises from within Christianity itself.

The second point is that, contrary to some modern opinion, this document is not written primarily with a missionary intention (in the sense that it was deliberately designed to make Christianity appear more acceptable to the Hellenistic world), but is addressed in the first instance, as are the epistles, to the Church of its day for 'the edifying of the saints'. The heart of it is pastoral and homiletic, not propagandist. It could be entitled, 'What the spirit saith to the Churches'.

The reality of the basic facts about Jesus, his birth, baptism, and so on, does not seem to have been in question before the era of gnostic speculation. That the Fourth Gospel has nothing to say on some of these historical facts is not likely to mean that there was any doubt on the part of the compiler that these events had taken place. But if we now consider the way in which the Fourth Gospel deals with the historical element in the authentic Gospel document, the facts about Jesus which were the common heritage of the Church, then the differences are notable. The birth, baptism, institution of the supper, are not given any place in their own right; the crucifixion, resurrection and parousia are not given the same connotation as they have in the Synoptic Gospels.

It cannot be maintained that this was due to oversight or lack of space. If the intention was to write a gospel—another of the same kind as the Synoptics—these historical facts were indispensable. As to space, the non-gospel material amounts to at least one third of the total document. We can only say that in the compilation important matters of known fact are omitted or realigned to give preference to the non-gospel material. This is another argument in favour of the theory that this non-gospel material was the original inspiration for the compilation of the Fourth Gospel.

The *Gospel of Mark* begins with the baptism of Jesus. If we accept the Proto-Luke hypothesis or something like it then the basic document in *Luke* begins here also. There can be little doubt that the known story of Jesus' life started from this point and this, of course, is what we should expect since at this juncture his life became public.

But in addition to this it is also beyond doubt that the earliest doctrine of his Messiahship was to the effect that at baptism he was endowed with his Messianic status. Thus doctrine and history converge to give unique significance to the baptism as the effective beginning of Messiah's career. He became Messiah at a specific time by the descent of the Spririt on him. As it was later expressed, he became Messiah by God's election and his own choice.

The opening chapters of *Matthew* and *Luke*, however, show that in many quarters this was not an adequate analysis of the historical and doctrinal position except at the initial stage. Historically and doctrinally it was of interest to ask, What of his life prior to baptism? While the historical question was not capable of being answered except in terms of legend, the doctrinal question could be, since it was not a matter of fact but of conviction.

At all events we have the two semi-legendary accounts of the birth of Jesus, each of which imports into his origin elements which in *Mark* belong to the baptism. What this implies doctrinally is that Jesus was born Messiah and did not become Messiah. The baptism now signifies his initiation into the public role of Messiah, not his initiation into the Messianic office.

But the Fourth Gospel records neither the birth nor the baptism. It opens with a philosophico-theological poem whose purport is that the eternal Logos became flesh in Jesus. This is not a denial that the birth and baptism took place but a statement which relegates both in view of the thesis that Jesus is the eternal Son who did not become but always is. The relation of those who believe in him is not in virtue of historical events but because of what and who he is, even if this has become known in a historical context.

The direction in which the writer's thought travels is probably, in view of the position of the non-gospel material, from the present quality of the relation of Jesus to believers to the nature of Jesus, rather than in reverse order. The theory is a consequence of the fact rather than vice versa. Because time does not affect the fact of the relationship with Jesus (he is present with his own always), it is not to be regarded as a primary factor in his nature. He did not become anything in time except *sarx* and, as we have seen, *sarx* is not the source of his significance.

The omission of the institution of the Supper (though not the meal itself) is notable in the Fourth Gospel. Again, this cannot be because it was not known or recognised as instituted on the night of betrayal, but because it is not given the same consequence as in the Synoptic Gospels.

As the birth and the baptism are not theologically the beginning of the uniqueness of Jesus, so the Supper is not theologically the prelude to his end. The memorial of Jesus' last days and in particular his death, which was the original significance of the Supper, is not regarded as a hallmark of discipleship because it is a binding of oneself to the past and to events, neither of which bears within itself the possibility of an immediate life-giving relationship.

In chapter six the Fourth Gospel gives a new meaning to the meal. It is not remembering the Lord till he comes but feeding on the bread of life. That is to say, the essential reference is not to either a past or projected event but to the fact of the union of Jesus and the believer. Again there is the displacement of a historical element by the new emphasis on present Christian experience. The Supper is not abolished but its origin and meaning are refashioned.

When we turn to the parousia, the same phenomenon is evident. The Fourth Gospel exhibits an ambiguity regarding the second coming which has often been remarked and explained in various ways. There are definite references to the last day and the resurrection at the end of time, but also teaching to the effect that whoever believes now has eternal life and has already passed through resurrection, because Jesus is now the resurrection and the life.

It is possible to argue that the passages referring to the resurrection at the last day are the work of a redactor who wished to bring the document more into line with the Synoptics in this respect. (Note that it is never suggested that the conflicting view is due to redaction). A good case is made out for the work of a redactor by G. H. C. Macgregor[1]. He would see some Baptist references and some of the Peter incidents in the Fourth Gospel as due to this motive.

It is worth quoting at length what he says about the latter.

R (the redactor) wishes to bring the Gospel more into line with the Synoptic tradition, and in particular to restore to Peter something of the prestige which he enjoys among the Twelve in the Synoptics. In XXI.1-14 R reverts to the Galilean tradition according to which the Risen Jesus appeared to the disciples not only in Jerusalem, as in our Gospel, but also in Galilee. This readjustment was particularly necessary on account of the Gospel's concentration of interest on Jerusalem. Moreover, R reintroduces the Galilean tradition in such a way as to re-assert the leadership of Peter. The story of the miraculous draft of fishes, which in Luke V.4-11 is related in connexion with Peter's first call, is here transferred to post-Resurrection days in order to add colour to the new commission now given to Peter, and so to correct the impression, which might be gained from the body of the Gospel, that Peter was subordinate to the Beloved disciple. Two points should be noted. First there is the close connexion of R's additions with Synoptic material. The resemblance both in thought and in language with Luke V.4-11 can hardly be accidental. Secondly, when we turn from the Appendix to the body of the Gospel, we shall again note how often disarrangement of the text and dislocation of the argument (phenomena, of course, most suggestive of redactional interference) are found in close proximity to passages which

[1] G. H. C. Macgregor and A. Q. Morton, *The Structure of the Fourth Gospel*, pp. 58 f.

reflect R's peculiar outlook as revealed to us in the Appendix, and which, in some cases also show traces of Synoptic colouring.

It is in connexion with the passages concerned with Peter that R's desire to adjust the Gospel to the Synoptic tradition is most manifest. The original source possibly contained no account of Peter's confession of Jesus as Messiah, and almost certainly none of the Denial. R accordingly seeks to make good the deficiency. To assign all these passages to R might appear to be too drastic if they did not display so clearly the infallible marks of R's handiwork—Synoptic colouring accompanied by apparent disarrangement of the text.

Macgregor goes on to examine in detail the confession (6.66-71), the denial passages (13.36-38; 18.15-18, 24-27) and certain passages dealing with John the Baptist which he also assigns to the redactor.

Macgregor's analysis may be well founded, but the point remains that it was not a matter of consequence for the compiler of the Fourth Gospel to deny the historical tradition of the Synoptics. He was not engaged in rewriting and correcting the story of Jesus but in emphasising a way of thinking about the relation between the living Lord and his disciples.

Therefore (to return to the parousia), it is probable that there was no wish in the circle from which the Fourth Gospel emanates, to deny the second coming any more than there was previously to deny the historical birth and baptism. It was a question of emphasis and not of outright antagonism, of affirming the one rather than denying the other.

In reference to the post-crucifixion area, the Fourth Gospel takes the same position as in reference to the pre-crucifixion area, that is it emphasises the priority of the eternal presence. The early gospel proclaimed a Jesus born, baptised, crucified, now in heaven ready to return and fulfil the hopes of his people. The Fourth Gospel portrays a Jesus who comes from God, lives on earth and returns to heaven, so that he can be spiritually and eternally present with his own. In the one case the story begins on earth, is translated to heaven and will have its climax on earth again at a future date. In the other, it begins in heaven, descends to earth and is crowned by a return to heaven, an already accomplished and continuous event which guarantees that Christ abides with his disciples for ever.

In the primitive gospel, Jesus' return to earth is to be the final proof of his divine commission and is the reason for his being Messiah in the first place. In the Fourth Gospel, his ascension to Heaven is the final proof of his eternal Sonship, his return to the glory which has always been his and from which he will not again be separated. Men will seek him and will not find him (on earth, either in earthly or Messianic guise) because he has returned for good. But he will send the Paraclete, his *alter ego*, the one brought into the scene in another form that is nevertheless fully representative, to be continually present with believers. This has results far exceeding those which flowed from the form of his earthly presence. He must go from sight that he may come to faith. His return is only to receive his own to his place, that where he is they may be (Chapter 14.3).

In this setting the resurrection of Jesus is not the prime historical event by which he will be able in due course to accomplish his mission; neither is it the proof that he is Messiah who will come again. It is the return of the Son to the Father, guaranteeing eternal life to his disciples and the presence that abides forever.

As regards the crucifixion, so central to early Christian doctrine, it is described in historical terms as in the other gospels but with modifications of fact. The ante-dating of the crucifixion (and the Supper) cannot have been unintentional. The tendency today is to prefer the Fourth Gospel to the Synoptics in this respect, thus giving the deliberate nature of the discrepancy the significance of historical trustworthiness which only more accurate information could justify.

This may indeed be so. But, in view of the way in which other historical events are handled in the Fourth Gospel, there may be another explanation—the modification of the place which the crucifixion and the doctrine associated with it had attained in the thinking of the Church at that time. If it can be allowed that the antedating of the Supper may be a way of saying, 'This must not be regarded as a Passover meal', then the antedating of the crucifixion which follows may be a way of saying, 'This is not a Passover event and ought not to be regarded as an atonement. Christians are not related to Jesus as Jews are to their sacred historical institutions'.

What Jesus gave, according to the Fourth Gospel, was not his death but his life, his willingness to become flesh, his total existence on earth. As E. F. Scott[2] says, 'The sacrifice was his appearance in flesh, and death did not add anything that was essential'.

Again, it is true that some countenance is given to the demoted view. The Baptist speaks of Jesus as the Lamb of God and the crucifixion in Fourth Gospel took place when the Paschal lamb was slain. C. F. Burney argued that *amnos* (lamb) is a mistranslation of the aramaic word for 'son' or 'child' and that the Fourth Gospel makes nothing of the coincidence in time of the slaying of the Paschal lamb and the crucifixion. In any case the Paschal lamb was not an expiatory sacrifice. But these qualifications apart, the point is that it would be consonant with what we have seen in other respects for two divergent views to be acknowledged, while at the same time no doubt is left as to which is to be given preference.

In the Synoptic Gospels the cross is viewed with fore-boding and, up to the prayer in Gethsemane, is potentially

---

[2] E. F. Scott, *The Fourth Gospel*, p. 208.

avoidable. It is the work of wicked men which God over-turns in the resurrection. It is accepted by Jesus after an agony of indecision, endured with a cry of desolation, necessary as a ransom for many.

None of these facts receives the same prominence and most are omitted from the Fourth Gospel account. There is no apprehension in view of the cross, no agony in the garden, no cry of dereliction. The cross is no charade, of course; it is encountering the hour and the power of darkness. But there is no doubt of the issue and no question that, like everything in the life of Jesus as far as the Fourth Gospel is concerned, it is comprehended in the purpose of God for the glorification of the Son and his exaltation to the glory he had left. In all this the co-operation of the Son is complete. When he says, 'It is finished', it is the work of his earthly existence that is over. His death is not an atonement but the conclusion of what began when *ho logos sarx egeneto*.

In all this, therefore, the Fourth Gospel is challenging the Church to make a choice since it is at a crossroads of its own history. This choice has many implications but it is essentially between a religion which will become moribund because it lives in the past and a religion that is constantly being renewed by the Spirit.

If there was a danger at the end of the first and the beginning of the second centuries that the Christian faith would become moribund, because it tended to be reduced to dutiful remembrance of Jesus' words and deeds in the past and the vague and diminishing hope of his future parousia, this emphasis on the power and freedom of the life which Jesus gives because he is the ever-present Lord was the word for the hour. Religious experience, the present union with him who is the Lord and giver of life, takes precedence over tradition in the form of past history or past theology. It is dynamic and creative. It cannot be bound by the forms and formulae of the past.

The question arises, How then could a document having at its core such a dynamic, liberating, anti-traditional principle, come to be regarded as itself the pattern for a new and more stringent tradition in which history and theology take precedence over the immediacy of religious experience? For this was what happened once the Fourth Gospel was accepted as authoritative in the Church.

The distinct and autonomous Christian Church was the outcome of a process which began with a Jewish sect cherishing Jewish traditions. The principle of the presence of Jesus had played a crucial part in freeing the faith, not only from its Jewish trammels, but also from the early traditions of history and doctrine which tended now to smother the creative impulse that came into being with the historical presence of Jesus. Nevertheless the Fourth Gospel, which embodied this liberating principle, became the most effective stereotype of a new tradition. 'The authoritative formularies of the Church's faith are stamped with the impress of St. John's Gospel', says R. H. Lightfoot, and he means the creeds which have been virtually unquestioned up to the present time. Both the necessity for credal uniformity and the content of the great creeds are related to the Fourth Gospel more than to any other document in the New Testament canon.

If we are to understand this development, it is necessary to remind ourselves that the Fourth Gospel is a compilation of unique complexity. It was ostensibly a gospel yet it is composed of elements which were either not present at all in the synoptic (i.e. prior) type of gospel, or not present to anything like the same degree.

There is, firstly, the non-gospel material which has been sufficiently characterised above. While the normal gospel's concern is to report the past and so, indirectly, affect the present, this material is primarily designed to affect the present directly. In the one case what is told is what Jesus said and did; in the other what he now says and does.

The second important element has to do not with the content of the document but with the degree of credence which it demands. Here the Fourth Gospel is pre-eminent. It gives the impression that it is the work of an intimate apostle or at least is vouched for by an intimate apostle. It is immaterial for our present purpose how or why this impression is created.

None of the Synoptics refers to any authority. Two came to be regarded as the work of men known not to be apostles and the third is only indirectly associated with the name of an apostle, not one of those thought to be most intimate with Jesus. In other words, this later document, the Fourth Gospel, claims to be regarded as trustworthy, first-hand testimony and thus unique.

Thirdly, and most important for our present inquiry, the teaching of Jesus in the Synoptic Gospels arises from the historical circumstances of his life in first-century Palestine, but the teaching contained in the Fourth Gospel is only incidentally associated with a historical context. In fact the subject of the teaching element in the Fourth Gospel is Jesus himself in his eternal Sonship. This means that the impression given by the Fourth Gospel as a whole is that it is a thesis on one theme, that it propagates a theology of Jesus which confers on him an unsurpassable status. Thus from a theological point of view the Fourth Gospel is distinctly superior to the synoptic tradition.

These differences were likely at first to make it difficult for the Fourth Gospel to be accepted in a situation in which the synoptic type of gospel was normative. We know that initially there was a strong objection to the Fourth Gospel on the ground of its divergencies, both historical and theological, from the Synoptics. But it is obvious that, should the Fourth Gospel once be accepted by the Church as worthy to be read, these differences would very soon ensure that it would be not simply one gospel among others but the supreme gospel. It claimed the highest apostolic authority. It was therefore most likely, on its own premisses, to be historically true. It gave Jesus a more exalted status than the other gospels did and indeed provided a theology which could not be transcended.

These advantages, of course, were to come into their own only towards the end of the second century and thereafter. That is to say, they were effective after the intention present in the non-gospel material had been realised. The Christian faith had already been liberated from Judaism and from its own primitive history. Consequently this element was allowed to fall into abeyance and the other elements, apostolicity, historicity and theological superiority, became the reasons why the Fourth Gospel was cherished and attained unique authority in the Church.

The Fourth Gospel became the key book for the true history of the life and words of Jesus and for the final theology of his nature and work. The canon of orthodoxy which the Church devised for itself was in terms which arose from the theological presuppositions of the Fourth Gospel. The heresies condemned by the councils which formulated the authoritative creeds were in effect condemned out of the Fourth Gospel.

If at the outset the document could have been ignored or suppressed, no doubt it would have been. But having survived to become accepted, it could only thereafter be idolized. The early commentators like Clement ('a spiritual gospel') and Origen ('the first fruits of all gospels') already gave it unique homage. They saw something of its power to liberate from the dead hand of the past but were captivated by its susceptibility to the subtle allegorical interpretations in which they excelled. They have been followed through the centuries by an innumerable company who have vied with each other in extolling the Fourth Gospel, mostly for the wrong reasons and principally (a) as true history and (b) as final theology.

This continues into our own time. Referring to the commentators of the first quarter of this century J. H. Bernard[3] writes, 'Scholars have devoted themselves rather to the historical and critical problems of the gospel according to Saint John than to the exposition in detail of the text'. Bernard's own introduction devotes 108 out of 175 pages to the same problems and none directly to the message of the non-gospel material. Even a frankly devotional commentary like that of W. Temple[4] can be written only on the basis of the historical reliability and theological supremacy of the document.

Clearly, from the time that the Fourth Gospel was accepted in the Church it was its value as guaranteed history and unimpeachable theology that was extolled. Of that element in it, which was a force against convention, tradition and enslavement to the past, a powerful instrument in favour of spiritual religion and spiritual freedom, nothing more was heard. The book was not only adopted into the establishment but elected to the highest place therein. Who now would dare to suggest that it started out as a passionate anti-establishment tract for the times?

The Church was therefore condemned or rather condemned itself to be obsessed first of all by the need to defend the apostolicity and historicity of the Fourth Gospel against all comers and, secondly, because the Fourth Gospel had given more to the creeds than any other New Testament document, to expounding the theological presuppositions of the Fourth Gospel as the climax of Christian theology, the only sufficient and final theology of the Christian Church for ever. The Church has therefore persisted in treating the

[3] J. H. Bernard, *St. John*, Vol. 1, p. CLXXXVII.
[4] W. Temple, *Readings in the Fourth Gospel.*

Fourth Gospel as a gospel, which it was not except in form, and has expounded a final creed on the basis of a document which took its origin from the thesis that there can be no such thing.

From the beginning scholars had been led into absurdity by the necessity to maintain that what this document said must be true in the literal and historical sense and also the bearer of another sense which only the enlightened can discern and which is present even where the plain sense is plain nonsense. Origen even maintains that the things in this document which do not make sense when interpreted literally, obviously demand to be spiritualised, that even gross discrepancies which would discredit any other document are designed in this case to yield spiritual truth which can be preserved in material falsehood. For Origen all numbers and place names have hidden meanings and the most platitudinous statements conceal spiritual revelations. While Theodore of Mopsuestia is content to comment on the seamless robe that this was a common method of weaving in those days, Origen sees it as an allusion to the wholeness of Christ's teaching. The same method enables Cyprian to see here a reference to the unity of the Church and Cyril of Jerusalem to find wonderful confirmation of the doctrine of the virgin birth. Unhappily such absurdities are not confined to the early centuries.

The Fourth Gospel soon became the greatest literary treasure the Church possessed. It was cherished for two reasons: (1) as the most trustworthy account of the actual words and deeds of Jesus, indeed the only account of his most significant words and deeds, and (2) as the fount of wisdom regarding the central doctrines of Christianity, and the person and work of Jesus the incarnate Word. These converge to give the purpose for which the book was written, according to the early commentators and to all orthodox commentators ever since, namely, to display the divinity and deity of Jesus. Strangely enough, as Wiles points out, the early commentators did not make use of John 20.31 for this purpose.

Early commentators are concerned almost exclusively with what the gospel teaches about the mystery of Jesus, the God-man, incarnate Son of God and second person of the Trinity. To them the figures of light, bread, the vine, the shepherd, are interesting for what they tell us about the nature of Christ. They are oblivious of the fact that originally the message was what he means to those who believe in him. Truth came very soon to be equivalent to orthodoxy which is, of course, right notions about Jesus' divine nature. Believing comes to have a meaning which is not that of the original writer; it is now the ability to credit certain divine propositions.

We may say therefore that the Fourth Gospel was accepted and idolized because its original *raison d'être* was forgotten and because it was made to bear interpretations which in some instances were clean opposite to those of the original writer. It was not intended as a source of historical data. It was not originally designed as a canon of orthodoxy. On the contrary, it was a message of prophetic fervour to the Church at the beginning of the second century. It was a blast against the whole notion of orthodoxy and in favour of inward and spiritual freedom. But even the portions that give the document its similarity to a gospel can hardly have been intended to serve the purpose of an intellectual creed.

The Fourth Gospel does include the Prologue and it does set out a way of thinking of Jesus as the Son who came down to reveal the Father, believing that this was a truer way of thinking of Jesus than as Messiah who would return at the parousia. How far the writer of the non-gospel material, or the original thinker behind it would have concurred in this it is not possible to guess.

The compiler, however, must have been aware that his

book was pioneering a new way of thought, a daring thesis
at odds with the generally received tradition. He could hardly
have regarded himself as part of a doctrinal establishment or
ever have wished to be such. If he believed that the central
fact about a Christian is that he is in personal, present communion with the living Jesus (and this was what had been
learned from a beloved teacher whose teaching he wished to
perpetuate), is it possible that at the same time he thought an
intellectual grasp of theological propositions was even more
important?

It is the theologian's delusion that the Church survives
because of the correctness of its theology. The believer, as
distinct from the professional theologian, knows that the
Church lives because of the devotional quality of Christian
living, because of Christian fellowship, because of the Christian's compassion for the sins and sorrows of mankind, in
short, because of what the Fourth Gospel would call the
degree to which Jesus is present and abides in the life of
individual Christians.

It is religion which is timeless, not theology. The importance of the Fourth Gospel in the life of the Church (as
distinct from its interest to the minds of scholars) resides in
the fact that it has elements which evoke a realisation of the
timeless and therefore present reality of religion. Elements
that call for belief, in the Johannine sense, rather than for
comprehension or intellectual assent. This the simple believer
has always grasped.

The tragedy of the fate which overtook the Fourth Gospel
in Church history is that the timeless element tended to be
ignored and the elements which belong to the age in which
it was compiled to be promoted to the highest place. And
this has persisted to the present day. In the matter of inter-
preting the message of the Fourth Gospel, few are prepared
to regard the document as a composite work and this puts a
premium on the traditional evaluation of the book. Fewer

still are prepared to consider the Logos theology as a brilliant but historically conditioned *tour de force*. The suggestion that the Fourth Gospel was issued as a protest on behalf of living religion, against the soul-destroying influence of a theological system which is bound by the history and traditions of the past, and for the priority of the direct relation between God and the soul, will no doubt still appear to many little short of sacrilegious, exactly as the Fourth Gospel itself seemed to be to some of its early readers.